Poetry across the Curriculum

Poetry across the Curriculum

New Methods of Writing Intensive Pedagogy for U.S. Community College and Undergraduate Education

Edited by

Frank Jacob
Shannon Kincaid
Amy E. Traver

BRILL
SENSE

LEIDEN | BOSTON

All chapters in this book have undergone peer review.

The Library of Congress Cataloging-in-Publication Data is available online at http://catalog.loc.gov

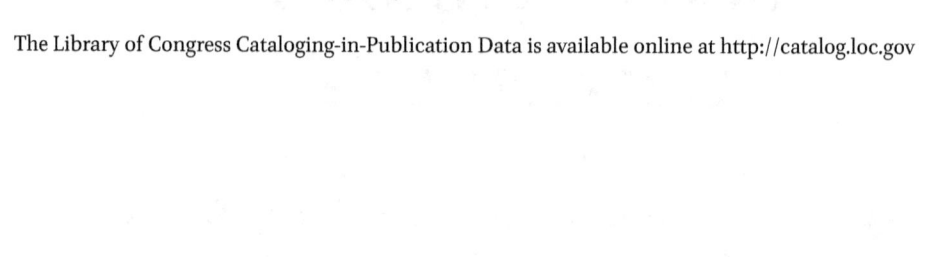

Typeface for the Latin, Greek, and Cyrillic scripts: "Brill". See and download: brill.com/brill-typeface.

ISBN 978-90-04-38065-3 (paperback)
ISBN 978-90-04-38066-0 (hardback)
ISBN 978-90-04-38067-7 (e-book)

Copyright 2018 by Koninklijke Brill NV, Leiden, The Netherlands.
Koninklijke Brill NV incorporates the imprints Brill, Brill Hes & De Graaf, Brill Nijhoff, Brill Rodopi, Brill Sense and Hotei Publishing.
All rights reserved. No part of this publication may be reproduced, translated, stored in a retrieval system, or transmitted in any form or by any means, electronic, mechanical, photocopying, recording or otherwise, without prior written permission from the publisher.
Authorization to photocopy items for internal or personal use is granted by Koninklijke Brill NV provided that the appropriate fees are paid directly to The Copyright Clearance Center, 222 Rosewood Drive, Suite 910, Danvers, MA 01923, USA. Fees are subject to change.

This book is printed on acid-free paper and produced in a sustainable manner.

Contents

Introduction
Pedagogy and Poetry across the Disciplines   VII
   Frank Jacob and Shannon Kincaid

PART 1
Arts

1   "Object Poetry" as a Source of Inspiration for Design Studies   3
   Ravid Rovner

2   Arts Integrated Learning through Poetry
   Implementing Awareness, Metaphor, and Play across Curriculums   25
   Alison Cimino

PART 2
Biology

3   Poetry in a Biology Classroom   43
   Urszula Golebiewska

PART 3
English

4   An Initiation into Academic Discourse with Poetry   55
   Susan Lago

5   Poetry and Student Learning   71
   Angela Hooks

6   "Thirsty Women and Fuckboys"
   Teaching Shakespeare with Memes   82
   Kathleen Alves

7   In Deference to Dreams Deferred
   Langston Hughes' Poem, "Harlem (A Dream Deferred)" and Its Application across the Curriculum   98
   Alice Rosenblitt-Lacey

PART 4
History

8 Expressive Content Writing
   The Inclusion of Poetry in Undergraduate History Courses   115
      Frank Jacob

PART 5
Philosophy

9 Pedagogy in Verse
   A Philosophical Approach to Poetry across the Curriculum   131
      Shannon Kincaid

10 Empowering Poetic Defiance
   Baudelaire, Kant and Poetic Agency in the Classroom   141
      Joshua M. Hall

PART 6
Sociology

11 Contextualizing Math and Poetry in Community College Courses
   Impacts and Implications in Introduction to Sociology   161
      Amy E. Traver

   Index   175

Introduction
Pedagogy and Poetry across the Disciplines

Frank Jacob and Shannon Kincaid

> Today in our public schools the activity of education
> is in the nature of a dynamic group concern
> with the verities of group living.
> The curriculum is no longer accepted as a body of standardized content
> possessing essential values and validities,
> but rather for its social implications and consequences.
> From an educational end, the curriculum has become a social means.
> LEON MONES, "Poetry in the social curriculum," *Junior-Senior High School Clearing House* (1935: 203)

∴

In 1935, Leon Mones, an English teacher at the Central Commercial and Manual Training High School of Newark, New Jersey described highschool education as a means of addressing social issues. A lot has changed since then, and as education at all levels is becoming more and more STEM oriented, it very often loses sight of its "social implications," especially since curricula have to predominantly be success- and job-oriented. Those who demand "modern curricula" today are now no longer demanding "social implication and consequences" but a measurable outcome for a possible income, which provides financial promises for possible students. The students, and, of course, administrators alike seem therefore to be less interested in a solid education in the humanities, regardless of the fact that such disciplines do promise measurable outcomes as well (Bradburn & Townsend, 2016). However, as Patricia Meyer Spacks and Leslie Berlowitz wrote in 2009, "the humanities remain alive and well—despite inadequate funding, insufficient jobs, and widespread misunderstanding of what, exactly, humanistic study involves and offers to society" (Meyer Spacks & Berlowitz, 2009: 5). While "the chronic underfunding experienced by the humanistic disciplines" (Ibid., 6) remains unchanged, discussions about the use and need for an education in the humanities continue, leading the Japanese Ministry of Education to demand the closing of humanities and social sciences programs in 2015, "after universities were ordered to 'serve areas that better meet society's needs'" (Grove, 2015). Likewise, in March 2017, President Donald Trump also proposed to eliminate the governmental endowments for the arts and the humanities—NEA and NEH—EH and 2017, Preside (Deb, 2017).

These trends should not only worry faculty members teaching in the arts, humanities, and social sciences, they should also worry anyone who understands the "social means" and overall value of such an education. This value should be discussed in more detail to highlight the essential need for the humanities and social sciences in any form of a good education. Education in general follows specific agendas and the curriculum can be used, to quote Richard Pring, as "a 'tool' to impart knowledge, skills, attitudes and behaviour, which the government or anyone in power believes to be important—especially in what is broadly conceived to be political education" (Pring, 1999: 71). Through courses in the humanities and social sciences, students tend to get in touch with what Printon calls "the voices of poetry, of history, of science, of philosophy ... [and] politics" (Ibid., 74) and are therefore educated toward possessing a critical mind, which supposedly helps them to make up their own opinions about current events.

A solid education in the humanities and social sciences consequently needs "the poetry, the novels, the dance, the media presentation, the arts, the historical accounts, the social interpretation, the theological analysis" to create and stimulate "the transaction between teacher and learner, and between the learners themselves as they examine critically those issues of supreme personal, social and political importance: sexual relations, social justice, the use of violence, the respect (or disrespect) for authority, racism, and so on" (Ibid., 83). However, the educational system has drifted away from an emphasis on social interaction and the liberal arts towards a focus on individual achievement in a narrowly prescribed curriculum. To put it simply, one might also argue, that a society that abdicates a humanistic education might also actively relinquish its collective ability to engage in critical thought and action on these issues. Of course, one has to be careful with generalizations, but the trend of an orientation towards a more STEM-based education is primarily driven by the values of capitalist interests and economically driven administrators do very often not consider the loss of discussions between and across the disciplines, which are most relevant for social progress as well (Goddard, 2016).

Poetry, as a method of teaching, is one such form of "discussion" that is currently at risk. As Nancy Martin Bailey wrote in 1989, "in an increasingly technological society, where the necessity for a curricular emphasis on the skills of mathematics and the thought processes of science is obvious, the literary arts, and especially the seemingly esoteric play with words that is poetry, could easily be squeezed out of the curriculum on the grounds of being irrelevant and frivolous" (Bailey, 1989: 51). The antagonism between the natural sciences and the the humanities might also be based on a simple hypothesis that political scientist Sheila Tobias expressed during a summer seminar at Cornell University in 1988, in which 14 engineering professor had to go through "an interesting week of poetry": "the scientist is just as uncomfortable with humanistic studies as the humanist is with scientific study" (Peterson, 1990: 396). While the humanities, however, still seem to be able to resist a trend that began many decades before, and especially in the United States is related to an increasing anti-intellectualism, poetry lost a lot of its public appraisal, most visible in book stores, where poetry is leading a rather niche existence. While far from dead, the humanities in general, and poetry in particular, therefore continue to struggle with a long-standing bias against creative expression and inquiry beyond narrowly prescribed disciplinary boundaries.

Poetry is usually confronted with the quite common accusation and "blunt assessment," (Niles, 1998: 143) that nothing is created by it. Fortunately, "The art of poetry has not always been practiced at the margins of society ... [and] [i]n some times and places, it has been a prized activity conducted close to the centers of social power." What "could aptly be described as functional speech of a highly wrought, privileged kind" (Ibid.) therefore provides, by evaluating its acceptance rate, a possible measure for the intellectual status of a society—something that currently is rather troublesome, considering the language level of the short messages of one of the highest political authorities in the United States. In contrast to the assumptions that poetry is an expressive writing form that can help to measure intelligence, it can be better used as an emotionally expressive language in many ways by many people, e.g. Hip-Hop. Furthermore, some poetry is also written and intended to expose the creativity and vibrancy and subversiveness of language, or to act as a social mirror. De facto, poetry played a very important role in human history and development, particularly during the German enlightenment, something Wolf Lepenies and Barbara Harshav highlight: "In the poet, humanity found its highest expression. And since all the potentials of the poet were conjoined in harmonic completion in Goethe's work, he epitomized a world view which-in Herman Nohl's description-preferred genius to rules in art, prophet to dogma in religion, hero to convention in ethics and the creative force of the people to all systems and theories of law and politics" (Lepenies & Harshav, 1988: 118). In 2004, Ivan Brady, Distinguished Teaching Professor and an anthropologist at the State University of New York, Oswego, declared the resistance of poetry against social neglect to be unbroken: "The poets march on, taking two principles of language very seriously: meaning is unlimited and everybody has some. So we say to the tinhorns: Kill and eat all the poets you want. We'll make more—in the underground, in our hearts, our thoughts, our stories, and the backrooms of our academies. And when the sun comes around again, look for us" (Brady, 2004: 636).

Poetry has a fundamental value, especially in the classroom. According to Beryl M. Parrish, poetry, like many other forms of literature, "makes alive and comprehensible to us the myriad ways in which human beings meet the infinite possibilities that life offers" (Parrish, 1956: 370). In addition, poetry also has a scientific value, which American literary critic George Steiner describes as being "a knot of words compacted with every conceivable mode of operative force" (Steiner, 1980: 32). Following a simile used by Nancy Martin Bailey, the scientific value of poetry can not be denied, as "For poets, words are like atoms with an irreducible nucleus of meaning orbited by a constellation of energized forces, both positive and negative" (Bailey, 1989: 52). In addition, Thomas S. Eliot (1888–1965), one of the great poets of the 20th century, described poetry as "the vehicle of feeling," (Eliot, 1985: 21) which makes it a valuable tool for teaching across disciplines, since "the challenge is deciding what kind of imaginative space one has to occupy in order to appreciate the qualities provided by these words in this order" (Altieri, 2001: 261). To decipher the letters, the "building blocks" (Ibid., 262) of a poem, and to give them meaning is a task that can be integrated into many courses in the humanities and social sciences, as well as in the STEM-related fields.

Teaching through poetry, however, does not always have to mean teaching poetry, but using poetry in the classroom can stimulate a positive response by students and educators alike, as the above quoted Leon Mones was already able to report in 1935:

> The poetic experience, whether in creator or reader, does not evolve from the logical responses standardized in conventional language, but from an organic readjustment to images and relations that effects new patterns of perception and vision. Mental and emotional residues in more or less subconscious and neutral states, in response to some catalytic urge, become suddenly dynamic and conscious and, in the resulting interplay, assume recreation in new patterns of relation. This is the poetic experience and, with modifications, the experience that underlies all types of creation before they become shared as public property in verbalized public language. (Mones, 1935: 204)[1]

This transformative process is essential for teaching any subject in the humanities or social sciences through poetry, but analytical skills, as they usually are demanded in STEM fields, can also be positively stimulated through poetry, because "the specific skills used in reading poetry ..., like the skills of mathematics and science, ... are essential to the full development of the individual" (Bailey, 1989: 51).

While poetry has been used for scientific research, e.g. poetic inquiry (Prendergast, 2009: 543–544), it is, of course, "an effective teaching resource" (Moran, 1999: 110). Any form of literature usually has the potential to be integrated in the classroom, where it provides a connection between curricular content and "real life" experience (Ibid., 111). Like many other forms of literature, poetry "presents students with alternative means of social interpretation other than through strict social-scientific inquiry" and it "can provide legitimacy to the course material in the form of corroborating evidence and add meaning to processes of social change, thereby enhancing students' comprehension of scientific analysis" (Ibid.). The poetry experience in class might also provoke a "new sensitivity to the unfamiliar" whole enhancing "a heightened understanding of the more familiar" (Ibid., 112). What is good for students and instructors alike is the emotional level they might reach together while discussing a specific poem, as the course might then lead away from the content-based lecture based teaching to a more interactive and emotionally-impacted form of understanding. Poems seem particularly helpful in stimulating or even provoking an emotional response by students in the classroom (Harker, 1978: 73).

Poetry, furthermore, forces the reader to "restructure his [or her] concept of reality to bring it into conformity with the reality embodied in the poem" (Ibid.). One could consequently argue that the poem provides more room for interpretation and therefore might be a more suitable textform to involve students in the process of finding its meaning. In contrast to a newspaper article, which provides clear information for a specific moment in time, poems are timeless and open to interpretation. In abstraction to natural science, one could follow W. John Harker's explanation:

> while the scientist is concerned with modeling the natural world with increasing precision and accuracy to produce higher levels of scientific prediction, the poet is concerned with modeling his own unique, imaginative response to the external world. And his poem stands both as a result of this modeling process and, in its construction, as an external illustration of the cognitive modeling process itself. (Ibid., 76)

The poem therefore expresses a "conceptual model of reality" and due to this task is forced to use a different form of language, one the students have to engage with on a deeper level before analyzing the meaning. Teaching through poetry is based on this process, and it is safe to assume that a poem is a better text form to cause student interaction with the material and the provided information per se.

Following Heidegger's thoughts, art and poetry "express truths that cannot be known in rational ways" (Pike, 2004: 27), and as the students do, we, i.e. humanity as a whole, "can understand Being through art" (Ibid., 28). Reading poetry provides access to this basic form of understanding, which is important for every student, no matter if that student is majoring in the humanities or social sciences or in a STEM field. It is reading and feeling poetry that makes us human, and that is why, no matter what career opportunities a final degree might provide, the teaching and the study of the humanities is crucial to the development of ethical practitioners of all disciplines. It is correct, to follow the past President of the Mathematical Association of America, Francis Edward Su, in his evaluation of poetry as a teaching tool. Su claims that "human beings [are] empowered to express their passion through poetry" (Su, 2010: 760) and this passion is needed for any kind of success in any kind of academic field. Especially a successful education can and should be based on poetry across the curriculum as well.

A large number of academic texts highlights the possibilities for the use of poetry in different fields of teaching (Robertson, 1997: 7–10; Spatz, 1982: 674–684). The fields or goals for which poems can be used in the classroom are limitless. From explaining geographic concepts (Kane & Rule, 2004: 658–659) to a better and deeper understanding of historical events and "revealing the complexities of a historical moment" (Meadows, 1999: 36),[2] poetry is a valuable tool. Some instructors also "consider poetry perfectly compatible with science," and they are correct (Kane & Rule, 2004: 659). Gil Abisdris and Adele Casuga emphasize this compatibility, when stating that "The language of science is metaphorical in nature. Due to the nature of certain abstract concepts, metaphors are used constantly by scientists to help them understand and conceptualize knowledge .... Scientific models are essentially equivalent to the metaphorical language used in poetry" (2001: 59). For students, to deal with poetry, especially when it comes to writing it themselves, provides a "difficult—and often intimidating—task" (Yahnke, 1981: 71), but once students engage with the material, it might not be hard for them to adjust, as Robert Yahnke's experiment to teach Haiku in the humanities at the General College (University of Minnesota) has shown. At the community college and undergraduate level, the use of poetry across the curriculum can be very fruitful and stimulating, however, some factors, like the objective aims of science and subjective experience of the humanities, have to be considered.

In contrast to Lesley Wheeler, Henry S. Fox Professor of English at Washington and Lee University in Lexington, Virginia, whose "talented English majors ... know just to do when handed a poem: read it with painstaking attention to textual detail and apply technical jargon to its features" (Wheeler, 2010: 207), students at American community colleges are usually arriving underprepared

INTRODUCTION   XIII

and many have never intensively dealt with poetry before (Chen, 2017).³ Therefore, one can not expect the students to have the skills to do a poetry analysis like Wheeler's students would be able to perform it. However, for our pilot study in the humanities and social sciences, it was not teaching poetry, but teaching through poetry that we sought to achieve. Three courses in History, Philosophy, and Social Sciences were designed to focus on the use of poetry in the classroom and compared to a control group, whose members took the same class but were not confronted with poetry. This pilot project at Queensborough Community College of the City University of New York, which took place in 2016/2017 and was sponsored through a Center for Excellence and Teaching Challenge Grant, was the initial step toward this edited volume.

In March 2017, a workshop was held at the college to broaden the perspective of instructors at Queensborough Community College in general, and the participating investigators of the pilot study in particular, on the use of poetry across the curriculum within different disciplines.⁴ Colleagues from English and Biology at Queensborough Community College, as well as colleagues from English at St. Johns University and LaGuardia Community College of the City University of New York, and from the department of Art and Design History at the Holon Institute of Technology in Israel, joined us for the workshop, and were able to further increase our understanding of the possibilities to use poetry as a textual pedagogical tool in the classroom. The chapters presented in the present volume are the outcome of the workshop and the discussions we had, and they present the options to use poetry in courses across the disciplines.

The Contributions

The following chapters provide insight into the almost limitless possibilities poetry provides within the classroom across disciplines. In the first part, dealing with the arts, Alison Cimino discusses "Arts Integrated Learning through Poetry" from an English professor's perspective, while Ravid Rovner frames poems as a source of inspiration for students taking classes in design studies. Both show how interdisciplinary approaches based on the use of poetry enrich the teaching methods in or with regard to the arts.

In the second part, to show that not only the humanities and social sciences can gain from poetic experiences by students and professors alike, Urszula Golebiewska provides insight into her experience using poems in the Biology classroom and how poetry before had helped to encourage her own scientific career in a STEM discipline.

The third part, which deals with English as a discipline, shows how poetry can positively impact the experiences and performance of community college and undergraduate students in many ways. While Susan Lago discusses poetry as a form of initiation into academic writing, Angela Hooks analyzes this specific text form with regard to student learning. Kathleen Alves and Alice Rosenblitt-Lacey then provide detailed case studies of their experiences of teaching Shakespeare with memes and integrating Langston Hughes' poem, "Harlem (A Dream Deferred)," across the curriculum.

As mentioned above, lyrical texts are particularly valuable to trigger emotions related to historical events. In the fourth part, Frank Jacob analyzes the use of poetry as a form of "expressive content writing" in different history courses within and outside the previously mentioned pilot study at Queensborough Community College.

In the fifth part, Shannon Kincaid discusses a "philosophical approach to Poetry across the Curriculum," sharing his results and findings in the philosophy classroom during the pilot study, and Joshua M. Hall evaluates the value of poetry in such a teaching environment by referring to Baudelaire, Kant, and the discourse about poetry with regards to philosophy.

Finally, Amy E. Traver contextualizes math and poetry and their implications for introductory courses in sociology at the community college level.

All of these detailed discussions of material and classroom experiences show how much potential poetry possesses in all disciplines, how poems might stimulate positive learning outcomes, and how lyrics across the curriculum have the potential to further strengthen the overall education of students, who end their careers in higher education not only successful, but as well-rounded individuals with a critical and open mind towards their environment and towards society as a whole.

Notes

1 Bailey (1989: 52) expresses that similarly, when she writes: "Since poetry is a case of highly elliptical writing, it seems to me that readers of poetry must develop especially elaborate hypotheses about the meanings of poems. These guesses enrich poems far beyond their original boundaries; yet those boundaries remain important as readers are guided in their hypothesis building by poets' attempts to communicate some portion of an individual cognitive and emotional reality."
2 Especially for historical events like the Holocaust, the emotional trigger poetry provides seem to be extremely valuabe when teaching such subjects (Danks, 1995: 358–361).
3 For a student's experience report about "getting into" poetry at a community college see Day, 2013.

4 We would like to thank the Kathleen Landy, the Director of QCC's Center for Excellence in Teaching and Learning for the overall support during the project in general, and for the help with the planning and preparation of the workshop in particular.

References

Abisdris, Gil, & Casuga, Adele. (2001). Atomic poetry: Using poetry to teach Rutherford's discovery of the nucleus. *The Science Teacher, 68*, 58–62.

Altieri, Charles. (2001). Taking lyrics literally: Teaching poetry in a prose culture. *New Literary History: Reexamining Critical Processing, 32*(2), 259–281.

Bailey, Nancy Martin. (1989). The importance of teaching poetry. *The Journal of Aesthetic Education, 23*(4), 51–62.

Bradburn, Norman M., & Robert B. Townsend. (2016, November 27). Use data to make a strong case for the humanities. *The Chronicle of Higher Education, 63*(15). Retrieved December 19, 2017, from https://www.chronicle.com/article/Use-Data-to-Make-a-Strong-Case/238502

Brady, Ivan. (2004). In defense of the sensual: Meaning construction in ethnography and poetics. *Qualitative Inquiry, 10*(4), 622–644.

Chen, Grace. (2017, May 18). New survey shows community college students feel unprepared for the rigors of higher education. *Community College Review*. Retrieved December 20, 2017, from https://www.communitycollegereview.com/blog/new-survey-shows-community-college-students-feel-unprepared-for-the-rigors-of-higher-education

Danks, Carol. (1995). Using holocaust short stories and poetry in the social studies classroom. *Social Education, 59*, 358–361.

Deb, Sopan. (2017, March 15). Trump proposed eliminationg the arts and humanities endowments. *The New York Times*. Retrieved December 16, 2017, from https://www.nytimes.com/2017/03/15/arts/nea-neh-endowments-trump.html

Eliot, Thomas S. (1985). The social function of poetry. In Richard Jones (Ed.), *Poetry and politics: An anthology of essays* (pp. 17–28). New York, NY: William Morrow.

Goddard, Renea. (2016, September 20). STEM isn't 'smarter,' it's just more capitalist. *The Odyssey*. Retrieved December 16, 2017, from https://www.theodysseyonline.com/stem-isnt-smarter-just-more-capitalist?utm_expid=.oW2L-b3SQF-m5a-dPEU77g.0&utm_referrer=https%3A%2F%2Fwww.google.com%2F

Grove, Jack. (2015, September 14). *Social sciences and humanities faculties 'to close' in Japan after ministerial intervention.* Retrieved December 16, 2017, from https://www.timeshighereducation.com/news/social-sciences-and-humanities-faculties-close-japan-after-ministerial-intervention

Harker, W. John. (1978). Reading poetry. *The Journal of Aesthetic Education, 12*(4), 73–85.

Kane, Sharon, & Audrey C. Rule. (2004). Poetry connections can enhance content area learning. *Journal of Adolescent & Adult Literacy, 47*(8), 658–669.

Katy Day. (2013, June 4). Poetry: A community college student's perspective. *Howard County Poetry and Literature Society*. Retrieved December 20, 2017, from https://hocopolitso.org/2013/06/04/poetry-a-community-college-students-perspective-by-katy-day/

Lepenies, Wolf, & Harshav, Barbara. (1988). Between social science and poetry in Germany. *Poetics Today: Interpretation in Context in Science and Culture, 9*(1), 117–143.

Meadows, Doris M. (1999). African-American poetry and history: Making connections. *OAH Magazine of History, 13*(2), 36–41.

Meyer Spacks, Patricia, & Berlowitz, Leslie. (2009). Reflecting on the humanities. *Daedalus, 138*(1), 5–7.

Mones, Leon. (1935). Poetry in the social curriculum. *Junior-Senior High School Clearing House, 10*(4), 203–205.

Moran, Timothy Patrick. (1999). Versifying your reading list: Using poetry to teach inequality. *Teaching Sociology, 27*(2), 110–125.

Niles, John D. (1998). Reconceiving beowulf: Poetry as social praxis. *College English, 61*(2), 143–166.

Parrish, Beryl M. (1956). Teaching literature for social consciousness. *The High School Journal, 39*(7), 370–377.

Peterson, Ivars. (1990). Poetry lessons. *Science News, 138*(25–26), 396–397.

Pike, Mark A. (2004). Aesthetic teaching. *The Journal of Aesthetic Education, 38*(2), 20–37.

Prendergast, Monica. (2009). 'Poem is what?' Poetic inquiry in qualitative social science research. *International Review of Qualitative Research, 1*(4), 541–568.

Pring, Richard. (1999). Political education: Relevance of the humanities. *Oxford Review of Education, 25*(1–2), 71–87.

Robertson, Jackie. (1997). Poetry in science. *Voices from the Middle, 4*(2), 7–10.

Spatz, Lois S. (1982). Six women: A demonstration of the uses of poetry in health science curriculum. *College English, 44*, 674–684.

Steiner, George. (1980). *On difficulty and other essays*. New York, NY: Oxford University Press.

Su, Francis Edward. (2010). Teaching research: Encouraging discoveries. *The American Mathematical Monthly, 117*(9), 759–769.

Wheeler, Lesley. (2010). On capstones, service learning, and poetry. *Profession, 2010*(1), 207–219.

Yahnke, Robert. (1981). Teaching haiku poetry in the humanities classroom. *Improving College and University Teaching, 29*(2), 71–77.

PART 1

Arts

∵

CHAPTER 1

"Object Poetry" as a Source of Inspiration for Design Studies

Ravid Rovner

Designers know how to evaluate a product's cost, how to adapt a product to a need, how to create need, and how to make a product look desirable. While they are indeed more accustomed to working with visual imagery than with textual concepts, poetry is *entirely* outside the normal frame of experience for most designers. As a design professor in Holon Institute of Technology, I have noticed that many of my students are not used to reading poetry, and when inquiring with colleagues, I found that none of them had asked students to turn to poetry during their design process.

Nevertheless, poetry is an excellent tool for reflecting on one's profession, since the sense of unfamiliarity provoked by poetry compels one to examine familiar things in a fresh, non-prejudiced manner. Design students might gain much from encountering poetic form which deals with the objects of their research. Since the expression of the poetic form is textual, it might be considered as situated between art and theory; as an idea summarized or sketched in words. This feature might, very quickly and intuitively for creative people, provide an artistic yet non-visual perspective on the objects of study. Furthermore, there are similarities between the work of the poet and the work of the designer. As the American poet William Carlos Williams (1883–1963) phrased it: "We forget what a poem is: a poem is an organization of materials. As an automobile or kitchen stove is an organization of materials. You have to take words, as Gertrude Stein said we must, to make poems. Poems are mechanical objects made out of words to express a certain thing" (Wagner, 1976: 73). I therefore set myself to find a poetic reference to the world of design, that is, a form of poetry that deals with designed objects, such that design students, as well as design practitioners, can relate to and benefit from in their work. The well-known poetic genre of "Object poetry," dating back to the 19th century and gaining prominence in the 20th century focuses on man-made objects, among other types. As I have learned, 21st century poetry concentrating on man-made objects is, in many ways, dissimilar to traditional Object poetry.

In the following Chapter I describe what "Object poetry" is, discuss the differences between contemporary and traditional poetic expressions, and share various ways in which I implement designed-object poetry in Class. One key example is an exhibition I held at the HIT design faculty's gallery, "Vitrina," during the spring of 2016. The exhibition featured a collection of Hebrew poetry written over the past twenty years, with the sole focus of *designed* objects. The exhibition traveled throughout Israel and was presented in four additional establishments during 2016–2017. Another way of combining Object poetry in design studies was more direct, and included working with both students and faculty members in order to analyze the poems' typical characteristics and draw up the resemblance of poetry and design to which Williams referred. Still, one should not fail to notice the faculties of poetry that design could never possess, being an artistic expression that is first and foremost physical and visual. I hope to show that such methods contribute to design studies and praxis, and provide conceptual inspiration for designers and design students.

1   Object Poetry's First Steps

A recent definition of "Object poetry" is found in *The Poetry Dictionary* by John Drury (2006: 193–194). Drury defines an "object poem" as "a poem about an intimate object. It may give us a fresh look at something ordinary, or it may transform a strange object into something familiar" (Ibid., 139). He adds that "the term is a translation of the German 'Dinggedicht,' or 'thing poem' ..." (Ibid.). The examples Drury provides are of concrete man-made objects, e.g. Don Bogen's "Card Catalog," Charles Simic's "Fork," May Swenson's "A Navajo Blanket" and so on. But object poetry is neither limited to the concrete, nor to man-made objects. The history of object poetry reveals the variety of objects to which poets have addressed. An object poem can also be about a natural object, an animal or a landscape (Müller, 1997: 75). To give one example, some of Rainer Maria Rilke's (1875–1926) famous object poems include "Der Berg" (The Mountain) (Willard, 1965: 318) and "Der Panther" (The Panther, Eben, 1989: 633) among others. However, since the aim of this chapter is to discuss poetry that deals with man-made objects, I will refrain from exploring the vast scope of Object poetry, and will restrict the discussion to object poems that deal with designed objects.

The term "Dinggedicht" was introduced in 1926 by Kurt Oppert in his paper "Das Dinggedicht: Eine Krunstiform bei Mörike, Meyer und Rilke" (Oppert, 1926: 747). Oppert attributed the genre to the work of three great 19th century German poets: Rilke, who was mentioned above, Eduard Friedrich Mörike (1804–1875), and Conrad Ferdinand Meyer (1825–1898). The first Dinggedicht, attributed to Mörike and dated 1837, is titled "An eine Äolsharfe" (To an Aeolian Harp, Schier, 1967: 50):

> Leaning up against the ivy-covered wall
> Of this old terrace,
> You, an air-borne muse,
> A lute-melody full of mystery,
> Begin,
> Begin again,
> Your melodious lament!
> You come, winds, from far away,
> Ah! from the boy
> Who was so dear to me,
> From his hill so freshly green.
> On your way, streaking over spring blossoms
> Saturated with sweet scents,
> How sweetly, how sweetly you besiege my heart!
> You rustle the strings here,
> Drawn by harmonious melancholy,
> Growing louder in the pull of my longing,
> And then dying down again.
> But all at once,
> The wind blows violently
> And a lovely cry of the harp
> Echoes, to my sweet terror,
> The sudden stirring of my soul,
> And here, the ample rose shakes and strews
> All its petals at my feet![1]

This is an object poem first and foremost because it is devoted solely to one object. The poet describes the aeolian harp picturesquely, bewildered by the object's uniqueness. This type of poetry, however, was not only a German phenomenon. As early as 1820, English poet John Keats (1795–1821) anonymously published his "Ode on a Grecian Urn"[2]:

> Thou still unravish'd bride of quietness,
>   Thou foster-child of silence and slow time,
>   Sylvan historian, who canst thus express
>   A flowery tale more sweetly than our rhyme:
> What leaf-fring'd legend haunts about thy shape

> Of deities or mortals, or of both,
>   In Tempe or the dales of Arcady?
> What men or gods are these? What maidens loth?
> What mad pursuit? What struggle to escape?
> What pipes and timbrels? What wild ecstasy?[3]

In both the first stanza of "Ode on a Grecian Urn" cited above, as well as in Mörike's "To an Aeolian Harp," the poets address the object as if it were a person. They use the subject pronoun "you/thou" to address an inanimate object. Nevertheless, it is obvious that the poets do not confuse a lifeless object with a living one, let alone with a speaking subject. Moreover, the object does not stand for a missing subject. It is clear that the poets do not wait for or imagine a response. It is a way to emotionally express their enchantment and fascination with the beauty of the object standing in front of them. These two early Object poems were revolutionary, not only for dealing with a single object. The aeolian harp and the Grecian urn are both classical objects, relating to ancient Greece. Yet the poetic expression is typical to romanticism, which stood against the norms of neo-classicism. Thus, both poems reclaim the universality of Grecian art when using the object to reflect on the sensuous everyday in a non-temporal way.

The reference to objects of ancient time may be attributed much to the publication of the *Anacreontea*, a collection of sixty short poems written by different Hellenistic and Byzantine Greek writers, which imitated Anacreon's (c.582 BCE-c.485) poetic style. The collection was first published in French in 1554 by Henri II Estienne as the work of Anacreon.[4] It was later published in English in 1651 by Thomas Stanley (Flower, 1950: 146), and in German in 1846 by Mörike, who in 1835 began a thorough study on Greek poetry in order to translate it (Schier, 1967: 50). In the preface to his translation of Anacreon, Mörike notes that "the Anacreontea contains a series of representations, which have as their object some real or imagined works of art, some of which are for themselves small paintings, but without a truly personal motive" (Ibid., 51).[5] It is worthwhile to examine an instance of the compilation's odes, to comprehend Mörike's assertion and his inspiration. Ode XVII is titled "On a Silver Drinking Cup":

> Skilled Hephaestus, matchless wright,
> Crave me from this silver bright
> Neither arms nor panoply;
> Battles, wars, are naught to me.
> Fashion me a hollow bowl,
> Deep so that my thirsty soul
> In its depths my cares may sink

> When the grateful juice I drink.
> Grave me no fantastic forms,
> Nor Orion, star of storms;
> Neither let Boötes rise
> Nor the Wain nor Pleiades;
> What have I to do with these!
> Master, on the goblet shape
> Purple clusters of the grape;
> Let the wine-press, too, be trod
> By love's naked gold-tressed god,
> And let fair Lyaeus be
> Present at the revelry. (Anacreon, 1915: 79)

The elements of object poetry already exist in this ode: the poem deals with one object; the object's name is the poem's title or a part of it; the poem creates the feeling that the poet was looking at the object while writing, so the object is revealed before our eyes as the poem unfolds. But Keats' "Ode on a Grecian Urn" and Mörike's "To an Aeolian Harp" can be seen as exceptional compared to other 19th century object poems, which neglected the romantic expression of a subjective and emotional position toward the object. Instead they were articulating a somewhat sterile poetic picture, aiming at a more universal idea of the object. This also applies to object poems referring to ancient Greek and Roman objects, most famously Conrad Ferdinand Meyer's "Der Römische Brunnen" (The Roman Fountain) and Rainer Maria Rilke's "Archaïscher Torso Apollos" (Torso of an Archaic Apollo, Greene & Cushman, 2017, 224):

> We cannot know his incredible head,
> where the eyes ripened like apples,
> yet his torso still glows like a candelabrum,
> from which his gaze, however dimmed,
>
> still persists and gleams. If this were not so,
> the bow of his breast could not blind you,
> nor could a smile, steered by the gentle curve
> of his loins, glide to the centre of procreation.
>
> And this stone would seem disfigured and stunted,
> the shoulders descending into nothing,
> unable to glisten like a predator's pelt,

> or burst out from its confines and radiate
> like a star: for there is no angle from which
> it cannot see you. You have to change your life. (Rumens, 2010)

As with the other poems quoted above, the theme of this poem is a Grecian art object, and therefore is an example of ekphrastic poetry—poetry inspired by visual art, dating back to Homer's description of the Shield of Achilles in the "Iliad" (Moorman, 2006: 46). The poem is not romantic, but gives a more precise portrayal of the visual encounter of the poet with the object. This is apparent, among the rest, in the use of the pronoun "we" at the beginning of the poem.

It would be nevertheless misguided to either give the impression that object poetry is limited to a revival of archaic poetry, in theme or style, or that it first appeared during the 19th century. A prominent object poet in the middle-ages was the Jewish-Spanish poet Judah Halevi. Halevi, who wrote in Hebrew during the 12th century, dedicated several poems to everyday objects such as a picture frame, weighing scales, scissors, a mirror, a pen, etc. In some of his poems, Halevi did not mention the name of the object in the poem's title but rather at the bottom, creating a kind of poetic riddle. One such riddle-poem in a collection of five is titled "Klay Bayit" (Household Goods):

> And what is blind though its eye is in its head
> And is desired by all of creation
> What labors all its life
> To clothe others, but is itself naked.
>
> The Needle.[6]

Lacking the personal aspect altogether, this poem seems much more modern than the poems discussed above. Its style is straight to the point, aspires to accuracy and is highly concise, leaving the observer outside of the poem entirely. Halevi's poems might therefore be seen as predecessors to 20th century object poems, as will be explicated in the following section.

2   20th Century Object Poetry

Object poetry gained much popularity in the 20th century. Notable 20th century object poets include Francis Ponge (1899–1988) in France, William Carlos Williams (1883–1963), Gertrude Stein (1874–1946), Wallace Stevens

(1879–1956) and Marianne Craig Moore (1877–1972) in the United States, Juan Ramón Jiménez (1881–1958) in Spain and Pablo Neruda (1904–1976) in Chile, as well as Rilke, who outlived Mörike and Meyer.

The essential features of object poetry articulated above were met in the work of these poets, but they tend to practice greater poetic freedom and experimentation. As in the German "Dinggedicht," these poets were writing about things, each poem dedicated to a particular singular thing: be it an animal, as in Ponge's "The Wasp" or Neruda's "Ode To The Cat;" a natural phenomenon, as "A fire" or "A Father" in Stein's "Tender Buttons." While 19th century object poets were sometimes inspired by Ekphrastic poetry when drawing up their textual descriptions of ancient Greek and Roman works of art, 20th century poets were inspired by contemporary artists, and were creating object poetry anew. To give some examples, between 1906–1908 Rilke was influenced by Rodin's sculptures and Cezanne's paintings (Müller, 1997: 314); Stein was influenced by her friend Picasso,[7] and so was Ponge (Stamelman, 1978: 409). William Carlos Williams noted that his poetry was influenced by his mother's still life paintings (Dijkstra, 1978: 58).

Williams captured the new essence of object poetry in a phrase he coined in 1927: "no ideas but in things" (William, 1986: 263). His words mark a new and modernized view of poetry about objects, namely that ideas can appear only through concrete things, and not in abstract forms. Williams's most famous object poem is, perhaps, "The Red Wheelbarrow" (originally titled XXII) from "Spring and All" (1923):

> so much depends
> upon
>
> a red wheel
> barrow
>
> glazed with rain
> water
>
> beside the white
> chickens.
> (Williams, 1970)

Numerous studies have dealt with this poem, which is also considered a milestone in imagist poetry. There is a strong feeling of gazing at the red wheelbarrow while reading the poem. A different form of poetic expression can be found in Gertrude Stein's book from 1914, "Tender Bottons," which was a reaction of the poet to her encounter with plastic art. The book is divided into three sections: "Objects," "Food," and "Rooms," each containing many short poems in the form of descriptions, as if in some uncanny dictionary. To give one example from the section titled "Objects":

SHOES
> To be a wall with a damper a stream of pounding way and nearly enough choice makes a steady midnight. It is pus.
> A shallow hole rose on red. A shallow hole in and in this makes ale less. It shows shine. (Stein, 1997: 16)

The title of the poem is quite straightforward, but clearly, accuracy of description was not something Stein was aiming for. Instead, she was using words as Picasso used colors and shapes, playing with them, "walking," as it were, on the thin border between significance and nonsense. In Stein's words: "I made innumerable efforts to make words write without sense and found it impossible. Any human being putting down words had to make sense out of them" (cited in Schwenger, 2001: 103). So throughout the reading we are being tossed around in the reality the words create.

Picasso's influence on Ponge's poetry was different. As Richard Stamelman notes, "Ponge conceives of words as material entities which are as substantial and concrete as the objects they denote. In many instances there is a resemblance between the form of the thing and the shape or sound of the word which designates it .... For example, [in Ponge's "La Cruche"] there is the word "cruche" ("pitcher") whose middle vowel ("u") is surrounded on each side by a wall of consonants, thus graphically resembling the inner hollow of the pitcher which is itself surrounded by clay walls" (Stamelman, 1978: 411). So Ponge, unlike Williams and Stein, was using the visibility of the words, guided by their graphic appearance. As Ponge himself noted: "At every moment in the work of expression, as writing is progressing, language reacts, proposes its own solutions, incites, creates ideas, assists in the formation of the poem .... Each word imposes itself on me (and on the poem) in all its thickness, with all the associations of ideas which it contains" (Ibid., fn. 4).

Observing the great influence art has on object poetry, it is clear that object poetry can inspire designers in a dynamic circle: the designer created a pitcher, which the poet then described in a poem, which the designer can later read and interpret, and create another object, referring to the poem, and so forth.

3 Extracting the Characteristics of Object Poetry

Before understanding how designers may profit from reading object poetry, it is still essential to articulate the characteristics of object poetry, and to examine contemporary object poetry in their light. Firstly, as we have seen, object poems deal with only one concrete item and are wholly dedicated to it, while usually ignoring the relationship between that item and other objects. This aspect is fortified by the poet's choice to use the object's name as the title, in most cases with no additional words. This choice signals to the reader the idea that she is about to read a poem about that object.

Secondly, the poems have a descriptive character, even when the description is almost nonsensical (as in Stein's "Tender Buttons"). For these poets, describing an object is not about capturing its unique specificity, but about constituting a textual portrayal of the object matter. It is never a one-time object, but a canonical object, one that retains a shared form and meaning in "everybody's" mind. Ponge explained that his poems are "a [new] kind of writing which, situating itself more or less between two genres [definition and description], would borrow from the former its infallibility, its indubitability, and its brevity; and from the latter, its respect for the sensory aspect of things ..." (Ibid., 420, fn. 20).

Thirdly, Object poetry contains usually a non-emotional view of the object matter. The poet is the observer and speaker, but the poem neglects the subject's emotions toward the object, and is devoid of the poet's personality. It is about the objectivity of objects—the universality of the experience of the object by any subject: its canonical form as it exists in the mind of the so-called common person.

This leads us to the fourth attribute of object poetry: Its non-metaphorical approach to the object. The object never symbolizes anything—neither a person, nor anything else. It is the object itself that the poet wishes to describe. Therefore, in reading the poem, no secret meaning is hidden, and no interpretation is required on the reader's side. As Rudolf D. Schier phrases it, "... by definition, all Dinggedichte ["thing poems"] must strive toward the complete elimination of all interpretation." His claim is immediately followed by a positive assertion according to which "the aim is to describe the object with such precision, excluding all metaphor and all personal intrusion, that word and thing will be one, and the object will reveal Being itself" (Schier, 1967: 55).

The non-emotive, non-metaphorical view of the object is directed at showcasing the object's inner truth. As N. M. Willard describes it, "... they [the poets] are united by the desire to create a poetry based on the careful examination of concrete things as the way to attain poetic truth" (Willard, 1965: 311). It seems that the poets presumed that truth lay in the object, and that the poet possessed the ability to extract it via text. Martin Heiddeger described the notion of "truth put into work," meaning that a poem is wholly self-contained, so that it does not stand for anything beyond itself. The example he gives for this quality is Conrad Ferdinand Meyer's poem titled "Der Römische Brunnen" ("The Roman Fountain") (Heidegger, 1971: 37). The poems are about the concrete, simple and direct experience of the object, the sensory and not the intellectual idea. The poet captures the essence, the higher reality of the actual object, all the time being merely an observer, not a direct channel to the world of platonic ideas.

The fifth and last attribute of object poetry is the poem's transformation of the everyday common object into something remarkable, worthy of admiring. Examining Rilke's poems, Müller argues that "objectivity is, in … [Rilke's object] poems, not only the result of subject-matter (the world of things or objects), but also of method or technique … Subjectivity enters the poem by way of intense individual perception and rigorous artistic work which turns the object beheld into an art-object, …" (Müller, 1997: 80). The readers are spared of any distractions when entering the gates of the poem's title, and are forced to pay their full attention, and perhaps even admiration, to something as ordinary and common as a wheelbarrow.

4 Contemporary Object Poetry

An examination of many contemporary poems dealing with designed objects shows that a significant portion of them do not appeal to the characteristics stated above, besides, at times, the first one—the title—and the last one—transforming a simple object into a work of art.

Most importantly, contemporary object poetry does not assume that it is possible to take the subject out of the poem. On the contrary, the object always already incorporates the subject, either the one who made it or the one who uses it. The subject is never left out, he or she is always a crucial part of the object, and the desire—the passion, the emotional connectedness of the subject, the wish to possess, etc.—is the center of designed-object poetry. This idea is nicely captured in Daniel Oz's poem:

> A pale night falls upon my monitor
> Chat windows have swung shut
> Screen savers roll like sleeping eyes
> Dim light like velvet slides down ever more

Revealing the darkness of your hip
Only the vapor of your breath that clung unto my screen
Has yet to disappear. (Oz, 2013: 12)

In this poem, the poet's interlocutors are absent, represented by a computer screen—the conversation is replaced with chat windows, as so often is the case nowadays. Yet when the chat windows are turned off, the lover is revealed, dimly lighted by the computer's screensaver. The object and the subjects are interconnected—since the subject is exposed by the object. The poem is like a statement according to which an object cannot be understood without the presence of a subject.

In other contemporary Object poems, the object is an expression of personal emotions, which particularize the personal relationship of the poet with the object. Consider Roy C. Arad's poem "Against the Strainer," which opens with:

1.
This is a vehement condemnation of the strainer
A protest of its minuscule perforations
An uprising against its empty desire
I am principally opposed to the entire concept of a net
And the handle-ness of the red
Handle
And the place in which they come together
The lukewarm touch at seven p.m.
You are an upside-down mountain of nothing
The disgrace of the kitchen. (Arad, 2014: 14–15)

In the opening part of the poem, as in the three parts following it, the poet expresses his disdain for a strainer, which is said to have an "empty desire." The object it personified, which makes the reader wonder whether the strainer is a kitchen aid, or whether it stands for something else. Either way, the poet reveals a very personal sentiment.

Compare Oz's and Arad's contemporary object poems to "Soap" by Ponge, his well-known prose poem from 1967. The poem adheres to a man-made thing (soap), and even includes statements of desire. Nevertheless, this poem is concerned not with the poet's personal experience, but with the will to capture the "object's qualities." The desire is described as a property, not elaborated, not lingered upon. The soap is merely a soap, it is the thing itself; and the desire is constant and universal:

> Violent desire to wash one's hands.
> Dear reader, I suppose that you sometimes want to wash your hands!
> For your intellectual toilet, reader, here is a text on soap. (Ponge, 1969: 23)

In some poems, the subject emerges only for an instant. Consider "Fork," a poem by Serbian-American poet Charles Simic:

> This strange thing must have crept
> Right out of hell.
> It resembles a bird's foot
> Worn around the cannibal's neck.
>
> As you hold it in your hand,
> As you stab with it into a piece of meat,
> It is possible to imagine the rest of the bird:
> Its head which like your fist
> Is large, bald, beakless, and blind. (Drury, 2006: 194)

This poem carries all the attributes of a traditional object poem in its first stanza, but the second stanza reveals its personal attitude. The generality is replaced by the personal pronoun "you" who, along with a "large, bald, beakless, and blind" fist transforms the fork into an intimidating figure, thus turning the entire poem into a personal protest—against carnivores, perhaps, or against a specific person that only the poet knows.

Many times, contemporary object poetry deals with more than one object. The poems reveal the relationships between everyday objects in customary or uncustomary situations. This allows for a broader examination of objects in various settings, a vital concern for product and interior designers. Take, for example, Maya Bejerano's poem titled "Motion":

> Objects in motion:
>
> The spoon loses its spoon-ness
> The glass—its glasss-ness
> The garment—its garment-ness
> The chair—its precise chair-ness
> The cabinet—the honor of its cabinet-ness
> The pot—its pot-ness
> The fork—its ...
> The tablecloth—its pleasing tablecloth-ness

> The table—the honor of its table-ness
> The bed—its bed-ness
> The book—its book-ness, the library—its library-ness
> The dress loses its dress-ness
>
> Only the rags are joyous
> All are now equal and resemble them
> And only the clock remains constant. (Bejerano, 2001: 41)

This poem describes not only the quality of one object, but the transformation many objects undertake when set in motion, for example when moving into another house. Bejerano verbally describes a metamorphosis that is textual but can be also visual, and the reader is left to imagine the objects as they transform and lose their essence. Bejerano's clock "remains constant," but were it listed in the stanza above, it might have brought to mind the melting clocks in "The Persistence of Memory" by surrealist artist Salvador Dalí.

Like traditional Object poems, contemporary ones do not use the designed object as a simile, but unlike them, they tell us about an object in a seemingly ingenuous way, drawing a new metaphor. For example, in Ella Novak's poem, a broken salad container might seem like a metaphor for a dysfunctional relationship:

> The salad container
> we've been using for years
> has a crack
> and can no longer contain salad:
> The dressing will drip in the fridge
> or on me.
>
> Before I throw it away
> I wonder—
> Is it possible to use it as a flower pot?
>
> It is not. (Novak, 2010)

In today's narcissistic society, there is a constant need to reflect on how the object is incorporated into life—how it is both the product of designers and consumed by people. Nevertheless, not all contemporary object poetry has changed in the manner discussed above. Indeed, many contemporary object poems dealing with designed objects, adhere to the "Dinggedicht" tradition.

They were written recently, but since they address the appearance of the iconic-universal image of the objects, they could have been written in another time, by another poet of another origin. A much refined example is Malki Tesler's poem:

> Dark line
> Bright line
> Dark line
> Bright line
> Dark line
> Bright line
> Dark line
> Bright line
> A ladder. (Tesler, 2010/11: 22)

Similarly to Judah Halevi's riddle poems discussed above, the poem's answer is found in its end. Unlike it, the poem *visually* captures the essence of a ladder—as the phrase "dark line" is shorter than "bright line," the poem graphically simulates the fundamental appearance of the physical object. It narrows the essence of the object down to its bare necessities. Furthermore, it is read in a manner similar to that of a descending ladder: we know we've reached the ground only when the poem is over. It is an exceptional poem, since on the one hand, it has no subject, and on the other hand, it does not necessarily contain a truth, because the last line—the answer—could have equally been "a crosswalk," "a prisoner's uniform," "a comb," etc. This poem, in its slimness, nicely expresses an issue in contemporary design, where the neo-modernist demand to discard all "unnecessary" details nevertheless requires to retain one or more basic visual denominator in order for the user to correctly "read" the use of the object.

Perhaps more so than in poems dealing with universal concepts or feelings such as love, family, birth, etc., designed-object poems are susceptible to a cultural-linguistic reading. Upon reading, the designed objects take on their accustomed form in the reader's mind. Thus, a poem about a table napkin forms a defined mental image that is rendered quite differently by readers accustomed to eating at a Texan diner, a Neapolitan pizzeria, or a Tel-Avivian falafel joint. This fact is taken into account in many contemporary object poems. Consider Ronny Someck's poem, "Napkin":

> Time
> is as thin
> as a napkin wiping away

crumbs of words
from under the lip.
"Have you enjoyed yourself?" it asks. "Tell your friends."
"You haven't? Tell us."
And we, like the mouth, are never satisfied
with the menu of the body
and love at night's end
is a chair reversed
on a restaurant table.
Its legs in the air,
its head in clouds of floor. (Someck, 2009: 9)

The monologue of the napkin might sound strange to non-Israeli readers, however napkins printed with this slogan are a common thing in Israeli fast food restaurants. Via the poem, Someck creates a connection between an urgent need to feed the body quickly and cheaply, and a sexual encounter, in which the person is like "a chair reversed" in one of these restaurants, "never satisfied."

Designed objects can also have verbal connotations. "Coming out of the closet," for example, is a fairly universal image: in English as in numerous other languages, it means admit a secret, specifically that one is gay. But languages also have their own uniquely local "object slang," making the task of translating object poetry rather complex. As an example, in Roy C. Arad's poem "Against the Strainer" discussed above, a strainer is not only a kitchen sieve for the Hebrew speaker. It is also slang for a woman who doesn't answer phone calls. By playing on both meanings of "strainer," Arad creates a comic scene that evokes both human-object relationships and the poet's own personal experience.

5 Object Poetry for Designers

The contemporary examples of object poetry listed above provide a preliminary draft of the spirit and character of this renewed poetic type. The poet is not a static, anonymous observer. She brings into the poem the complex interrelations between a variety of common uses of the object and the verbal connotation it carries—globally and locally—to create a metaphoric reflection of an everyday state of affairs. Since the object in the poem is first and foremost man-made and man-consumed, it sheds light on human behaviors and lives.

All this is highly similar to the work of a designer. When a designer begins designing a product, she doesn't focus solely on a singular function the object has to perform. She studies the entire scope of the emotional relations and connotations that humans have when experiencing the item in a variety of common and uncommon situations. She also researches the functional and spatial relationships the product has with other products. Therefore, contemporary Object poets deal with similar issues designers face, only they end up with a different "product," since their materials are words. If poets examine designers' products and write about designed objects, why shouldn't designers regularly read poetry to reflect on their object of study? I believe designers could gain much from this activity, which broadens the scope of design research to the realms of the verbal abstract. As a design professor at the academy, a central question I confronted was how to share this insight with other designers, who were not used to reading poetry, especially young designers in the midst of their professional training. I decided to use the familiar designers' toolbox, and curate an exhibition that will familiarize designed-object poetry to designers.

6   Designed-Object Poetry Exhibition

The name of the exhibition I have curated, "Shirat Hafatzim" (object-Poetry), captures the essence of the poetic style. One Hebrew word for "object" is *hefetz* (plural: hafatzim), which, unlike the English *object*, carries the composite meaning of a physical object, a man-made artifact, and an object of desire. In other words, *hefetz* stands for a thing that one wishes to possess concretely— which is also the conceptual standpoint of (most) design schools of thought. The poetry presented in this exhibition, therefore, was not concerned with objects in general, but with the object as *designed*.

To provide a contemporary insight on how Hebrew poets articulate the designed world, the "Shirat Hafatzim" exhibition displayed poems written during the past twenty years. It included thirty poems in total, each one addressing daily issues faced by designers: modes of production and consumption, the impact of globalization on 21st century design, the relationship between a city and its inhabitants, how design contributes to violence, and more.

As seen in the examples above, the exhibition focused on the thematic aspect of the poems, imposing no constraints on form. The reason for this was that, beyond outlining the boundaries of designed-object poetry, the exhibition aimed to vitalize the connection between poetry and design and to establish the idea that writing object poetry is, in many ways, similar to design itself. Its goal was to present to designers, and in particular to design students, a new source of inspiration—one that they do not normally address or draw on in their work or in class.

One may ask: why create an exhibition instead of reaching poems where they're normally found, i.e., in books or on stage? Since young designers were the main target audience, an exhibition might provide a more intuitive first encounter with poetry than a book or a performance would. Still, considering the students' hesitation toward poetry (in design studies perhaps more so than in the humanities), merely posting the poems on a gallery wall might not suffice. To establish the idea that designed-object poetry can provide powerful inspiration for design praxis, more had to be done.

The design concept chosen for the exhibition was meant to convey the idea that a poem is itself a type of commodity. Each poem was laid out slightly differently on nonstandard paper (7x12 inches), giving it a singular look and emphasizing its independence. Each poem was printed in 2,500 copies, stacked into a back-glued tear-off pad. The visitor was able to tear off whichever poems he or she liked, and compile them into a special envelope provided at the entrance. The result was an individualized mini-anthology based on the visitor's personal choices. The act of choosing a poem and tearing it off mirrors the act of desiring an object and fulfilling this desire through action.

FIGURE 1.1   Students collecting poems in the "Vitrina" gallery at H.I.T, 2016

The stacks in the gallery formed a sort of three-dimensional graph, in which the gradual and uneven diminishing of the stacks reflects the desirability of the poems: the more popular a poem is, the lower its stack. To complete the experience, electronic screens offered the visitors a chance to listen to the poets reading out their poems. The experience of hearing the poems added an auditory dimension to understanding and participating in the exhibition; as well as an interpretational dimension, since the poems were being uniquely read aloud.

Additionally, Hezy Leskly's long poem "Holes and Handles" was hung on a wall. Leskly was a renowned Hebrew designed-object poet who died in 1994, so his poem was not read out by him, but was recorded at HIT's recording studio by 17 of my students. The visitors could follow the reading with a headset provided next to the display.

FIGURE 1.2   A student listening to "holes and handles" by Hezy Leskly

The exhibition was one result of my study of designed-object poetry in Hebrew, which—like Hebrew object poetry in general—had hitherto not been studied systematically. The study results were presented to my students in a course titled "Writing Design." Together we reviewed the poems, reflected on how each poem referred to one or more designed objects, and explored the differences between design and poetry as two aspects of aesthetics. For example, the experience of reading a poem is quite different from that of viewing an object. Poetry entails a linear procedure that reveals the object through reading, while (in most cases) a designed object is experienced instantaneously in its entirety. On the other hand, as I have already mentioned, *both* designers and poets express non-conventional takes on—and uses of—objects. As one of my students wrote: "You can do anything with a spoon/forget the butter knife/toast by clinking on your glass/spoonfully/...."

Following class discussion, students were asked to write their own object poems, using objects found in the faculty building: the garbage bin, the soft drink machine, the chair's writing pad, etc. This activity made them look at their surroundings with new eyes, turning it into an object for textual inspection, and forcing them to go beyond what is obvious about it. Afterwards, they were instructed to write poems as a preliminary phase of their design

research. As guidelines, they were given a list of questions to choose from, which directed them to the way contemporary poets address designed objects.
- What kind of relationships does the object has with other objects?
- How might a change in the object's surroundings affect it or the people using it?
- If the object had feelings, what would they be? How would it express them?
- How is the object's life cycle similar to or different from the human life cycle?
- And so on.

The results were always fascinating, as this task required students to poetically verbalize, rather than concretely visualize, their product. Some of the poems were published alongside well-known poets' works in the design faculty's online magazine, in a section titled "Designed-Object Poetry," stimulating further conversation on poetry as inspiration for design. This online section is still being maintained, as I continue to publish a new designed-object poem each week. Currently, this is the only stage dedicated solely to object poetry in Israel, and is perhaps quite unique worldwide.

During the exhibition, a festive poetry-reading event was held at the campus where a dozen of the featured poets read their poems. The event was documented in a short film by the students, in which they addressed the poets with the question "What is designed-object poetry?" The edited footage of the various reactions and comments by the poets was likewise posted in the design faculty's online magazine. This was another way of creating an encounter between these different artistic practitioners, designers and poets, both engaged with the same objective.

My main aim in this chapter was to argue that just as objects were and are a common source of inspiration for poets, so can poetry become a common source of inspiration for designers. The exhibition and the exercises given to students were just a first step in realizing this insight. Aside from providing the students with confidence in their ability to practice and enjoy poetry, these activities showed the students that there are other ways to look at the practice of design. It amplified the value of the written word, and showed how its connotative references and double-meanings can become powerful tools for innovative design. I also believe that designers can benefit from studying 19th and 20th century object poetry no less than contemporary object poems. As demonstrated above, object poetry has a highly rich history. It is the question of the stance the poet takes with regards to the object throughout history, that reveals the way societies have changed their relationships with the designed world. This historic apprehension is significant for students training to become professional designers. Reading designed-object poetry as a part of the history of design, writing object poetry as a natural part of the design process, preforming and discussing designed-object poetry in class, and many other viable courses of action, can become prevalent and costmary in design schools as well as in designers' everyday praxis.

Notes

1. Eduard Friedrich Mörike, "To an Aeolian Harp," trans. Emily Ezust. *The Lieder-Net Archive*. Accessed July 30, 2017. http://www.lieder.net/lieder/get_text.html?TextId=11618
2. Stephen Hebron, "An Introduction to 'Ode on a Grecian Urn': Time, Mortality and Beauty," *British library Online*. Accessed May 15, 2014. https://www.bl.uk/romantics-and-victorians/articles/an-introduction-to-ode-on-a-grecian-urn-time-mortality-and-beauty#
3. John Keats, "Ode on a Grecian Urn," *Poetry Foundation*. Accessed July 30, 2017. https://www.poetryfoundation.org/poems/44477/ode-on-a-grecian-urn
4. *Encyclopedia Britannica Online*, s. v. "Anacreon: Greek Poet." Accessed July 30, 2017. https://www.britannica.com/biography/Anacreon#ref167652
5. My translation.
6. יהודה הלוי, "כְּלֵי בַיִת," *פרוייקט בן יהודה*. accessed July 30, 2017 http://benyehuda.org/rihal/rihal6_11.html. Translated by Maayan Eitan.
7. *Poetry Foundation*, s.v. "Gertrude Stein." Accessed July 30, 2017. https://www.poetryfoundation.org/poets/gertrude-stein

References

Anacreon. (1915). *The anacreontea & principal remains of anacreon of teos, in English verse: With an essay, notes, and additional poems by Judson France Davidson*. London: J.M. Dent & Sons Ltd.

Dijkstra, Bram. (1978). *Cubism, Stieglitz, and the early poetry of William Carlos Williams*. Princeton, NJ: Princeton University Press.

Drury, John. (2006). *The poetry dictionary: With foreword by Dana Gioia*. Cincinnati, OH: Writer's Digest Books.

Eben, Michael C. (1989). Rainer Maria Rilke and Gertrud Kolmar: Das Dinggedicht—two poems. *Neophilologus, 73*, 633–636.

The Editors of Encyclopaedia Britannica. Encyclopedia Britannica, s. v. *Anacreon: Greek poet*. Retrieved July 30, 2017, from https://www.britannica.com/biography/Anacreon#ref167652

Flower, Margaret. (1950). Thomas Stanley (1625–1678): A bibliography of his writings in prose and verse (1647–1743). *Transactions of the Cambridge Bibliographical Society, 1*(2), 139–172.

Greene, Roland, & Cushman, Stephaen. (2017). *The Princeton handbook of world poetries* (pp. 215–255). Princeton, NJ: Princeton University Press.

Hebron, Stephen. (2014, May 15). An introduction to 'Ode on a Grecian Urn': Time, mortality and beauty. *British Library*. Retrieved July 30, 2017, from https://www.bl.uk/romantics-and-victorians/articles/an-introduction-to-ode-on-a-grecian-urn-time-mortality-and-beauty#

Heidegger, Martin. (1971). The origin of the work of art. In Martin Heidegger (Ed.), *Poetry, language, thought* (Albert Hofstadter, Trans., pp. 15–87). New York, NY: Harper & Row.

Keats, John. (1795–1821). Ode on a Grecian Urn. *Poetry Foundation*. Retrieved July 30, 2017, from https://www.poetryfoundation.org/poems/44477/ode-on-a-grecian-urn

Moorman, Honor. (2006). Backing into ekphrasis: Reading and writing poetry about visual art. *English Journal, 96*(1), 46–53.

Mörike, Eduard Friedrich. (1804–1875). *To an aeolian harp* (Emily Ezust, Trans.). The liedernet archive. Retrieved July 30, 2017, from http://www.lieder.net/lieder/get_text.html?TextId=11618

Müller, Wolfgang G. (1997). The transformations of the commonplace: Epiphanies in modernist object poetry (Rainer Maria Rilke and William Carlos Williams). In Andreas Fischer, Martin Heusser, & Thomas Hermann (Eds.), *Aspects of modernism: Studies in honour of Max Nänn* (pp. 75–95). Tübingen: Narr.

Poetry Foundation, s.v. Gertrude Stein. Retrieved July 30, 2017, from https://www.poetryfoundation.org/poets/gertrude-stein

Ponge, Francis. (1969). *Soap* (Lane Dunlop, Trans.). London: Jonathan Cape.

Rumens, Carol. (2010, November 15). *Poem of the week: Apollo's archaic torso* (Sarah Stutt, Trans.). *The Guardian*. Retrieved from July 30, 2017, from https://www.theguardian.com/books/booksblog/2010/nov/15/apollos-archaic-torso-sarah-stutt

Schier, Rudolf D. (1967, March). Natural objects and the imagination: Mörike's view of poetic language. *Modern Language Quarterly, 28*(1), 45–59.

Schwenger, Peter. (2001). Words and the murder of the thing. *Critical Inquiry: Things, 28*(1), 99–113.

Stamelman, Richard. (1978). The object in poetry and painting: Ponge and Picasso. *Contemporary Literature, University of Wisconsin Press, 19*(4), 409–428.

Stein, Gertrude. (1997). *Tender buttons: Objects, food, rooms*. New York, NY: Dover Publications.

Wagner, Linda Welshimer. (1976). *Interviews with William Carlos Williams: Speaking straight ahead*. New York, NY: New Directions.

Willard, N. M., (1965). A poetry of things: Williams, Rilke, Ponge. *Comparative Literature, 17*(4), 99–113.

Williams, William Carlos. (1970). *"XXII," spring and all.* S.I.: Frontier.

Williams, William Carlos. (1986). *The collected poems of William Carlos Williams, volume 1, 1909–1939* Walton Litz & Christopher MacGowan, (Eds.). New York, NY: New Directions Book.

Works in Hebrew

Arad, Roy C., (2014). *Noset Hametosim* (The Aircraft Carrier). Tel Aviv: Maayan. (Translated by Yardenne Greenspan).

Bejerano, Maya. (2001). *Hayofi Hu Kaas* (Beauty is Anger). Tel-Aviv: Hakibbutz Hameuchad. (Translated by Tsipi Keller).

Halevi, Judah. *Klei Bait* (Household objects). Project Ben-Yehuda. Accessed July 30, 2017. http://benyehuda.org/rihal/rihal6_11.html

Oz, Daniel. (2013). *Shyarei Ahava* (Remnants of Love). Tel Aviv: Even Hoshen. (Translated by Daniel Oz).

Someck, Ronny. (2009.) *Algir* (Algeria). Tel Aviv: Zmora-Bitan.

Tesler, Malki. (2010, November). "*.*" *Maayan, 6*. (Translated by Malki Tesler).

CHAPTER 2

Arts Integrated Learning through Poetry
Implementing Awareness, Metaphor, and Play across Curriculums

Alison Cimino

> Every word is a way out
> for an encounter often canceled,
> and it's then a word is true, when it
> insists on the encounter.
>   YANNIS RITSOS, *The meaning of simplicity* (1989: 25)

∴

Poetry arises from the liminal, the dreamtime, the in between. Yet to bring poetry to the page, to make it alive through reading or to bring it forth through writing, allows one to give language to the ideas that need space to breathe. Poetry allows people room to wander, to explore their own minds and fields of study. The benefit of using poetry in the classroom offers space for creativity by validating and honoring that learning itself is a creative affair (Duckworth, 1996: 12). Poets play with language, allowing the mind to make connections outside the usual prescribed conventions of thought and syntax. The language of poetry is the language of metaphor and imagery, available to students in their daily activities (Freeman, 2000: 253–281). In reading poetry, students discover and make meaning through cognitive connections. While many skills focus on analysis and critical thinking, both reading and writing poetry offer students the opportunity to slow down and work from their observations, the first step to analysis. Students notice the world around them when they write in imagery and metaphor; they step back from their usual thinking to observe and to reflect. By taking the time to write and critically unpack imagery and metaphor, students unlock the critical thinking skills needed to think creatively in Engineering, Science, Math and the Social Sciences (STEM) and other disciplines.

While many instructors advocate an inclusion of the arts by including a poem, song or occasional movement or visual activity in their curriculum, a fuller engagement with poetry—engagement with actively reading and writing poetry—creates a deeper learning experience for the student. In fact, by fully integrating poetry into the classroom the practice of reading and writing poetry will become more natural and beneficial; consequently, the critical reading and writing skills needed in these other fields will also be supported. Instructors should integrate the techniques of writing and reading poetry into the classroom through word play and by creating and decoding metaphor, simile, and figurative language. Through the emphasis of these creative writing skills instructors will foster critical thinking and creativity in students, aiding and supporting them across multiple disciplines.

My first encounter with arts integrated learning was as an instructor of poetry for Lesley University's Education Program, in the Division of Creative Arts in Learning. The program, a national master's level education program with cohorts across the country, works with teachers and administrators to integrate the arts into all content areas. While most of the graduate students are K-12 teachers, as graduate students, they fully participate in the art forms before creating lessons for their students. Educators take classes in visual arts, movement, drama, music, story-telling, and poetry, and the seminars are also arts integrated, so these same art forms weave throughout the entire program. While teaching poetry, I also learned from my students and colleagues how to integrate the arts through multiple disciplines. Later, I worked both as a Teaching Artist and Teacher Trainer through Lesley University and with grants from National Arts and Learning Collaborative and Very Special Arts while also teaching college writing, using these methods with first year college students, as I do at Queensborough Community College. These experiences are highlighted in this chapter which will explore the benefits of arts integrated learning through the use of poetry and play—specifically metaphor—across curriculums in higher education.

1   Arts Integrated Learning

Arts Integrated Learning attempts to introduce the various art forms: written, spoken, visual, auditory, and somatic through visual art, poetry, storytelling, music, theater, and dance, across curriculums. Through the arts, instructors have the capacity to invite creative thinking and seeing into their discussion of content. By integrating arts into curriculums, instructors have a greater chance of reaching various types of learners: visual-spatial, auditory, kinesthetic, logical, linguistic, interpersonal and intrapersonal (Gardner, 2017). In *Arts and the Creation of Mind*, Elliot Eisner cites John Dewy (1859–1952) to substantiate the necessity for arts integrated learning: "Experience is central to growth because experience is the medium of education. Education, in turn, is the process of learning to create ourselves, and it is what the arts, both as a process and as the fruits of that process, promote" (Eisner, 2002: 3). Arts integrated learning connects students to content through higher order engagement. Through poetry, students already have access to the artistic medium through language. Through the arts students can access their imagination and find an entry point into the content they not only study but help to create.

Arts integrated instruction generates a creative and active response to learning. Through imagination, instructors can cultivate and nurture higher order thinking. Elliot writes:

> Imagination, that form of thinking that engenders images of the possible, also has a critically important cognitive function to perform aside from the creation of possible worlds. Imagination also enables us to try things out—again in the mind's eye—without the consequences we might encounter if we had to act upon them empirically. It provides a safety net for experiment and rehearsal. (Ibid., 5)

Arts integrated learning honors the understanding that critical thinking and higher order thinking are creative. By having students read and write poems they are finding a creative outlet to connect to content. There is a higher likelihood of student involvement when students are invited to explore and to approach learning with creative curiosity. In arts integrated learning through poetry, students are invited to play with language through sounds, image, metaphor, and the poetic tools that they are already familiar with in their day to day lives. While arts integrated learning may be a recent pedagogical term, the ideas behind it have been discussed and forged about the imagination for many years.

In *Air and Dreams*, philosopher Rene Bachelard discusses the necessity to allow the mind room to wander and makes a case for poetry to reveal the imaginative condition. He cites poet William Blake who claimed, "The Imagination is not a State: it is the Human Existence itself" (Bachelard, 1988: 1). For Bachelard, poetry serves as the perfect medium to access imagination. Through the creation of poetic images, the poet "gives us his invitation to journey" (Ibid., 3). By its nature, the permission to wander, to construct and create, break the poet and the student poet out of habitual mind and into the realm of imagination. Bachelard writes, that "Habit is the exact antithesis of the creative imagination. The habitual image obstructs imaginative powers. An image learned in books, supervised and criticized by teachers, blocks imagination. When it has been reduced to form, an image is a poetic concept; it forms superficial links with other images" (Ibid., 11). Yet to create an image is to enter a space of engagement. Through the experience of the creative writing process, students create imagery and are offered another reference to a poem on the page: one of choice from a multitude of choices that the poet, like herself, has made. Bachelard's argument serves the creative process and honors the imagination.

2 The Benefits of Integrating Imagery and Metaphor

In "The Image," from *The Bow and the Lyre*, Octavio Paz (1973) addresses how the poetic image unites opposite realities and validates the accessibility of imagery and metaphor. He uses the comparison of children learning for the first time how one pound of feathers equals the same weight as one pound of stones to address the dichotomy that the poetic image can encompass. He writes,

> The poet names things: these are feathers, those are stones. And suddenly he affirms: stones are feathers, this is that. The elements of the image do not lose their concrete and singular character: stones continue to be stones, rough, hard, impenetrable, yellow with sun or green with moss; heavy stones. And feathers, feathers: light. The image shocks because it defies the principle of contradiction: the heavy is the light. When it enunciates the identity of opposites, it attacks the foundations of our thinking. Therefore, the poetic reality of the image cannot aspire to truth. The poem does not say what is, but what could be. (Paz, 1973: 85)

A means to connect opposites serves a valuable tool across curriculums. Through image, the poem aspires to connect to a deeper truth in the reality of the unsaid. While we know stones to be heavy and feathers light, we also understand the verisimilitude of circumstances bearing weight. As Kundera notes in his novel, *The Unbearable Lightness of Being*, at times the heavy —suffering, betrayal, even our own mortality—can bring with it a flash of insight or lightness, a moment of being where we can tap into the flash of joy in the human condition, against all odds.

The language of imagery and metaphor attempt to give voice to the ineffable. Students can access a place of understanding that they may primarily feel as inaccessible. Imagery, sensory details, and the objects that make up students' worlds, become the basis of metaphor. Through comparisons students develop an understanding and learn to articulate that understanding through metaphor. Later, Paz writes, "Feathers disappear in favor of a third reality, which is no longer stones or feathers but something else. But in some images—precisely the best ones—stones and feathers continue to be what they are: this is this and that is that; and at the same time, this is that: stones are feathers, without ceasing to be stones" (Ibid., 86). This metaphorical transformation empowers the poet to give voice to the dichotomies that exist in experience. Consequently, for students, poetry connects them to concepts and opposing concepts and helps them to identify these oppositions through language. The skills supported through metaphor and imagery also support the critical thinking and learning skills of STEM as well as the social sciences.

Science instructors and their students benefit by integrating metaphor, imagery and poetry in STEM classrooms, since poetry holds opposition through distilled language. In "The Use of Haiku to Convey Complex Concepts in Neuroscience," Alexia Pollack and Donna Korol note how medical students at UMass-Boston explored textbook models of addiction through haiku. Additionally, students reflected on their choices and wrote a brief explanation for their choice of imagery. The authors write, "The haiku helped draw forth the model's most salient features, which was aided by having more than one haiku representing each model" (Pollack & Korol, 2003: A42–A48). While some instructors may be concerned that students will be constricted by the form, many students are familiar with haiku, and the syllable count of 5/7/5 syllables for each line offers a simple yet challenging parameter for writing. The challenge of the form encourages students to think deeply about what they need to say and how they will connect to the imagery and metaphor that will effectively communicate.

One benefit of exploring poetic image across curriculums is that the critical reading of poetry invites the reader to explore layers and a multiplicity of meaning. As Paz writes, "The image does not explain: it invites one to re-create and, literally, to relive it. The poet's utterance is incarnated in poetic communion. The image transmutes man and converts him in turn into an image, that is, into a space where opposites fuse" (Paz, 1973: 97). Imagery, as opposed to a collection of things, invites multiple layers and interpretation, so that comparison—metaphor and simile—may generate and aid in understanding. Through imagery we connect with what we see and how we see. As imagery invites the reader and the writer to connect with the senses, a function that is readily available to students, it grounds students, readers and writers a like, in the natural world while connecting them to their higher selves. Paz notes the dynamic phenomena in the power of poetry:

Poetry is metamorphosis, change, and alchemical operation, and therefore it borders on

> magic, religion, and other attempts to transform man and make of "this one" and "that one" that "other one" who is he himself. The universe ceases to be a vast storehouse of heterogeneous things. Stars, shoes, tears, locomotives,

> willow trees, women, dictionaries, all is an immense family, all is in mutual communication and is unceasingly transformed …. (Ibid., 97–98)

For Paz, a diplomat and social activist, the interdependence and connections between people and the natural world would have been an important outcome for engaging in poetry. Through poetry people see themselves in each other and can tap into the interdependence of all living things. These connections are crucial in learning, as they foster a sense of empathy as well as a sense of community.

3   Cognitive Poetics and Accessing Language

A theory that acknowledges the need for arts integrated learning through poetry and supports it by its process is cognitive poetics. Cognitive poetics validates both the experience of the learner as well as the knowledge the text will bring to deepen understanding. Margaret Freeman, a pioneer in the field termed "cognitive poetics" by linguist Reuven Tsar, addresses the significance of cognitive poetics for both accessing and discussing poetry as well as creating poetry. To Freeman, the arts are a necessary and integral part of STEM education, and she is an ardent advocate of making "STEM" into "STEAM,"[1] by adding the "A" for the missing "arts or aesthetics." In "Poetry and the Scope of Metaphor: Toward a Cognitive Theory of Literature" Freeman writes:

> The theory I call *cognitive poetics* is a powerful tool for making explicit our reasoning processes and for illuminating the structure and content of literary texts. It provides a theory of literature that is both grounded in the language of literary texts and grounded in the cognitive linguistic strategies readers use to understand them. (Freeman, 2000: 1)

Cognitive poetics, an offshoot of cognitive linguistics, uses the same process of mapping that cognitive linguistics uses, only it applies it to poetry. Due to its primary concern with cognition and how we make meaning through observation, cognitive poetics is a contemplative approach to reading and understanding poetry. By mapping and making connections between patterns in poetry, cognitive poetics incorporates a mindfulness based approach. Similarly, the way cognitive therapy asks clients to observe their minds and thoughts—how we think and patterns of how we think—cognitive poetics asks readers to observe the patterns of language and how we create meaning with what is present on the page.

Cognitive poetics gives voice to how readers and writers articulate abstractions and ground their experience through metaphor. Through metaphor and comparison readers and writers find a medium to articulate experience by use of comparison. Freeman continues discussing the value of cognitive poetics by offering an apt description of its predecessor, cognitive linguistics:

> Cognitive linguistic (CL) theory claims that thoughts are embodied. That is, we conceptualize our ideas about the world and ourselves through our embodied experience of the world and self. That experience is constrained by the physical orientation of our bodies in space, by the constitution of our sense organs, by the repetitive neural synapses of our brains. Abstract ideas, like love, life, and the pursuit of happiness, are understood through the conceptual projection of physical experience. In other words, we cannot think abstractly without thinking metaphorically. Metaphor, according to CL theory, is not a matter of words but a matter of thought. (Ibid., 9)

Freeman's discussion of cognitive poetics, as steeped in CL theory, serves not only to support cognitive poetics in terms of discussing metaphor, but in using arts integrated learning through poetry as well. Cognitive poetics recognizes the basic ground of metaphor in common human experience and how that common experience makes poetry accessible. Freeman argues, we are used to using metaphor to understand abstractions like time. We use metaphor to communicate the human relationship to time and discuss time in terms of various metaphors: "time is an object: do you have *time* ... time *passed* quickly ... where did time go? or time is location: *Where* did you pass the time? Did you arrive *in* time?" (Ibid., 10). People, Freeman argues, are familiar with metaphor and use metaphor every day to interpret and communicate their understanding of abstractions. The argument serves arts integrated learning through poetry as well.

Students are familiar with metaphor—even though they may need some direction in identifying the metaphors they use every day. It is their familiarity with metaphor that serves as a ground for learning through metaphor. Since students are familiar with metaphor, having them draw and make connections through poetry is a small leap. STEM and social science teachers can also rely on this familiarity to ask students to create metaphors to understand the concepts crucial to their fields. As Freeman also notes, the same creativity that we want engineering and science students to possess in these fields can be accessed through poetry. Arts integrated learning through poetry successfully makes a body-mind connection with students by validating student experience.

4 An Invitation to Play: Integrating Poetry as Arts Based Instruction

Arts integrated learning serves students most when instructors also participate. When inviting students to engage with arts integration, instructors too must be willing to play. When I first began teaching for Lesley University's Division of Creative Arts in Learning, for their education course, The Language of Poetry, I learned first-hand how my own boundaries were inhibiting me from fully engaging in the process of learning. During my first workshop with seasoned arts integrated instructors I met my own resistance. At first, I stood stiffly in a corner of the room, arms folded, near the other poetry instructors, while the drama and dance instructors fully utilized the space around them for a warm up movement activity. Yet, once I allowed myself to move with the other instructors, to respond to the call and response through voice and movement, I realized the effect of somatic learning: as my body relaxed, my mind also relaxed.

I never would have called myself a kinesthetic learner until I experienced another workshop with Celeste Miller of Jacob's Pillow.[2] Miller, a choreographer and performer, demonstrated a science lesson exploring molecular energy through poetry and dance. Her movements told the story of learning about atoms while she created a dance that mirrored the frenetic movement of atoms. After she enacted the dance, she led us through movements, connecting our muscles to memorizing the movement and construct of an atom. Incorporating poetry with movement allows for distilled learning—images and metaphors make succinct connections to further assist memory. Even the most basic of movements paired with imagery and metaphor can have a pronounced effect.

Any image or line of poetry can be amplified and serve as a body-mind connection when combined with voice and movement. For example, when teaching Walt Whitman, known as "the body poet," I have students stand up and make a circle. I recite the following poem from "Song of Myself" and then have them repeat the first line: "I celebrate myself and sing myself," with their choice of tone, volume and movement. The class then echoes the same movement and intonation. While there may be students who do not wish to make a pronounced movement or loud sound, they too are invited to say the line as quietly or as demonstratively as they like. Even with a small handful of reluctant students, most students engage in the opportunity to try something different and to play. Through movement, the students enact a rendering of the poem as it becomes alive off the page. Another similar activity is to have students each read one line of a poem in their own way, again using intonation and movement while the class repeats each individual student's response.

Through these exercises, students meet the poem off the page and personalize it. The effect of repetition by reciting the poem aloud and with movement also serves as an exercise in internalizing the poem. Rhythm and language, off the page, enter both the space of the classroom and the bodies of the students as energy and vibration. Students are familiar with these rhythms, as much of poetry connects to the heartbeat. Students often make a further connection when they discover that iambic pentameter follows the heartbeat. To introduce this connection between meter and heartbeat, I have students tap out the lines of Robert Frost's poem, "Stopping by Woods on a Snowy Evening," while I recite the lines. We tap the unstressed syllables lightly over our hearts and tap the second stressed syllables with a stronger beat: "Whose *woods*/are *these*/I *think*/I *know*/Whose *house*/is *in*/the *vil*/lage *though*?" The exercise of feeling their own heartbeat with the heartbeat of the poem makes a body-mind connection to deepen the experience of the poem. By encountering the poem off the page through voice and movement, students also hear the poem and pay attention to the sounds of images and metaphors. The process of fully engaging with the poem also invites them to make the poem their own. This process facilitates and serves the creative process of writing poetry in response as well.

5 Arts Integration and Observation

While play and imagination are crucial to learning, the ground of creativity comes from observation. In "Apprehending Poetry" Lisa Schneier addresses the need to create a space for students to meet a poem on their own terms and to uncover meaning through observation. Many of the same skills used to scaffold the reading of poems can be implemented in writing poems. Reading Schneier's article changed the way I teach poetry. Instead of asking students to analyze what the poem "means," I follow Schneier's guidelines of having students read the poem (if possible, multiple times) and then discuss only what they "notice" before addressing what their observations mean. The process calls on students to make deliberate pathways between the text and interpretation. Through observation and repetition students learn to trust their own capabilities to discover meaning. Additionally, by asking students to "notice" and discuss their observations, students build confidence in their abilities as learners. Anyone can answer the question, "What do you notice," as the answer rests within the text. The exercise has the added benefit of encouraging students to use the text to support their own understanding of it. Therefore, the analysis of the poem becomes text based.

Additionally, students create meaning through an intentional connection to imagination. Teaching Artist Richard Lewis says, "Play is the force of much of the imagination" (*The Journey Within*, 1990). In *Taking Flight Standing Still*,

Lewis addresses the need for learners to connect to imagination to engage creativity: "We need to pay closer attention to the imagination as a source of understanding—and to listen more acutely to the centrality of imaginative thought and play in children—and its implication for our adult lives. We need to regain the poetry of learning, the surprise and delight ..." (Lewis, 2010). While Lewis mainly works in primary and secondary education settings, his ideas are echoed by college and graduate school educators who advocate for poetry in STEM classrooms: "The observation that scientists highly recognized for innovation are also artists supports the idea that the insight and creativity needed to generate scientific paradigm shifts may correspond to artistic creativity" (Pollack & Korol, 2013: A42–A48). The same observation skills used in discussing poems by literary authors also serves students when writing. For example, in science or writing classrooms students may write poems based on their observations. One exercise I incorporate in writing classes that also works with science lessons involves taking a walk and writing field notes based on observations. Students are told to create details based on up-close observations and from a distance, creating notes based on sensory observations. Later, these same observations become the basis for their landscape or nature poems. When doing this exercise with high school students, upon walking around their school and taking notes, the lesson took an environmental turn when students noticed the large amount of trash strewn around the campus.

6 Implementing Arts Integration Through Poetry in a History Lesson

Much of these arts integrated methods become synthesized in a history lesson I used with educators in the Lesley University Arts Integrated Learning Program and with primary and middle school students in history classes. While the lesson serves young students in primary schools, it also inspired the graduate students and can be altered to fit the needs of a college students. The lesson, "Coming to America," created by Poet and Teaching Artist, Mimi Herman, explores the immigration process of Ellis Island in 1901 though the creation of catalogue poems.[3] After learning about the history and immigration process of Ellis Island, students imagine what the experience was like then—and might be now—by assuming an identity of a person coming through Ellis Island in 1901. Herman creates identities and occupations for participants and organizes everyone by randomly handing out "passports" where each person will discover his identity, occupation, and family. The "family" then writes a group list or catalog poem by generating what they would need to bring with them for their new life. Students are directed to imagine they are packing one trunk.

They then discuss what they would bring. The acts of reading a sample poem, imagining and brainstorming what they would pack if they were leaving, and then writing their own poems deepens students' understanding and appreciation of history.

When implementing this lesson with graduate students at Lesley University's Creative Arts in Learning Education program, I incorporated the poem "Steerage" by Bert Stern, as the poem serves as an example of a list poem, as well as a poem that addresses the topic of immigration, though later in the century. The poem begins:

> Six apples my mother bought on the pier and wrapped in her shawl with
>   things we'd need every day.
> The things that we didn't—three linen napkins, a handful of silver spoons
>   my mother got from her mother
> when she married—these we kept in a hamper with handles we'd
>   schlepped up the steep plank.
> Steerage stank, even before we went down iron stairs with no railing.
>   Babies were crying.
> We looked back to the top of the stairs: a woman stood, looking down,
>   Frozen ... veh, smells of stale
> seawater and piss, animals and human sweat. *Gehenna* this woman cried.
>   But the crowd pushed behind her
> and she went down with the rest. Down there, at first, who knew where to
>   go the toilet, if there would be water? ... (Stern, 2009, pp. 7–8)

By reading and discussing the observations in the poem, students must consider what they will include as images in their own poems. While reading the poem scaffolds the activity of writing their own poems, the process supports the larger lesson of connecting with a historical and social moment. I encourage students to notice the sensory details of the poem, to consider how the poem evokes and communicates the emotional elements of immigrating, moving and leaving. Students discuss the tone of the poem and notice the way the speaker grounds the reader in both present and past places.

In discussing the poem, I ask students to consider the sensory details they notice. Smell offers strong imagery in the poem: "Steerage stank ... veh, smells of stale seawater and piss, animals and human sweat." Additionally, students observe the items the speaker and his mother pack and how these objects communicate identity. The sensory details, "babies crying," a woman calling "Gehenna," Hebrew for hell, even "Liberty like a tower," all locate the reader within the text and create emotional tension. By considering the sounds and smells of the poem, students connect in a visceral way with this moment in history.

Once students establish the images of the poem, they connect to the larger metaphor as well. The emotional tension in the poem heightens when the speaker creates the comparison for order through the simile:

> In a corner, on blankets, we made house: here, bundles to lean against,
>   there, to keep garlic and bread,
> sausages smelling of garlic, and just here, clean clothes to change into, as if
>   clothes could make order.
> At night I'd remember: in the market square Feter Joshua held me and said
>   he would come—
> in six months, no more. He talked to make order, he said what he hoped,
>   as if God gave us life
> as we want it. But order is like houses children weave from grasses, twigs
>   and leaves. (Ibid.)

Here, order is like "houses children weave from grasses, twigs and leaves," demonstrating the tenuousness our plans, and the fragility of our control. Later, order becomes conflated with "God" and "Liberty" as Stern continues,

> The first morning, for breakfast, my mother and I share an apple.
>   I closed my eyes, and saw
> the strong tower. I chewed as long as I could for the sweetness. When the
>   ship rocked,
> and over the thumping of engines the babies were crying
>   and women and men.
> crying to God for His mercy, I imagined America—Liberty like a tower,
>   her torch,
> father in a strong house, order. I said over and over,
>   *the Lord*
>   *is a strong tower*
>   *the righteous run into it*
>   *and are safe.*
> Up on deck each day we went heavier, until nobody lifted their head
>   up from steep plates of the deck
> and grey winches. Nobody talked. We could not look at the sea
>   or the dead sky
> above us. We hung between these. We would be here always.

Students recognize the emotional tension, as the speaker of the poem repeats "the Lord/is a strong tower/the righteous run into it." Through the metaphor, uttered as prayer, the poem heightens. Students connect with the empathic tension of the poem and consequently, with this specific historical moment.

The images of a ship and people cramped at the bottom of it ultimately also evoke the images of slaves who were forced into the country against their will. Each time I have worked with this poem, the images of bodies cramped in this confined steerage space, though the bodies of immigrants in the poem, always evokes the bodies of slaves and a discussion of slavery: those who chose to immigrate and those who were forced into slavery against their will. Through poetry, the historical conversation deepens, as students connect to other moments in history through the visceral images and metaphors of the text.

7 Conclusion

In "Thoughts on the Gifts of Art," Jane Kenyon advocates for the arts and poetry for their ability to connect us to imagination and our own humanity: "We cannot afford to ignore our inner lives, our imaginations, for when we do, we become capable of extreme cruelty and destruction. While poetry across curriculums assists students in learning *how* to observe and make connections through metaphor, poetry also connects to the *why* we learn. Poetry helps learners access the creativity and humanity behind all curriculums. Learning history, engineering, math and science become deeper experiences when connection to pathos. "Tenderness towards existence," in the poet Galway Kinnell's lovely phrase, "is what we lose when we lose art, or when we fail to value it properly."[4] While poetry instills in learners the capacity to connect with their humanity, it also has the propensity to deepen learning. Arts integrated learning offers multiple entry points of learning, as universal design advocates, to serve multiple learners. Introducing poetry and play across curriculums includes multiple art forms which then connect to multiple intelligences. Arts integrated learning through poetry honors and validates all types of learners. Additionally, the creativity generated by learning through reading and writing poems stimulates students' curiosity by making personal connections to content as well as allowing imagination to flourish. By inviting creativity across disciplines through arts integrated learning through poetry and arts integrated learning, instructors honor the creativity within their students and their own disciplines.

Notes

1. Conversation with Margaret Freeman, February 6, 2017.
2. Celeste Miller. Accessed October 15, 2017. http:/www.celestemiller.com/
3. Mimi Herman. Accessed October 15, 2017. https://www.mimiherman.com/
4. Jane Kenyon, *A Hundred White Daffodils* (St. Paul: Graywolf Press, 1999), 138.

References

Bachelard, Gaston. (1988). *Air and dreams: An essay on the imagination of movement* (Edith. R. Farrell, Trans.). Dallas, TX: The Dallas Institute.

Campo, Rafael. (2006). Why should medical students be writing poems? *Journal of Medical Humanities, 27*(4), 253–254.

Cowen, Virginia, Kaufman, Diane, & Schoenherr, Lisa. (2016). A review of creative and expressive writing as a pedagogical tool in medical education. *Medical Education, 50*(3), 311–319.

Duckworth, Eleanor. (1996). *The having of wonderful ideas*. New York, NY: Teachers College Press.

Eisner, Elliot W. (2002). *Arts and the creation of mind*. New York, NY: Yale University Press.

Freeman, Margaret H. (2000). Poetry and the scope of metaphor: Toward a cognitive theory of literature. In Antonio Barcelona (Ed.), *Metaphor and metonymy at the crossroads: A cognitive perspective* (pp. 253–281). Berlin: Mouton de Gruyter.

Freeman, Margaret H. (2005). Poetry as power: The dynamics of cognitive poetics as a scientific and literary paradigm. In Harri Veivo, Bo Pettersson, & Merja Polvinen (Eds.), *Cognition and literary interpretation in practice* (pp. 31–57). Helsinki: Helsinki University Press.

Gardner, Howard. (1983). *Frames of mind: The theory of multiple intelligences*. New York, NY: Basic Books. Retrieved from http://www.tecweb.org/styles/gardner.html

Herman, Mimi. (1990). *The journey within with Richard Lewis*. New York, NY: Renascence Films. Retrieved from https://www.mimiherman.com/

Kenyon, Jane. (1999). *A hundred white daffodils*. St. Paul, MN: Graywolf Press.

Lewis, Richard. (2010). *Taking flight standing still*. New York, NY: Touchstone Center.

Miller, Celeste. Retrieved from http://www.celestemiller.com/#/artist-statement/

Paz, Octavio. (1973). *The bow and the lyre* (Ruth L. C. Simms, Trans.). Austin, TX: Texas University Press.

Pollack, A. E., & Korol, D. L. (2013). The use of haiku to convey complex concepts in neuroscience. *Journal of Undergraduate Neuroscience Education, 12*(1), A42–A48.

Project Zero. Retrieved from http://www.pz.harvard.edu/professional-development/online-courses

Ritsos, Yannis. (1989). *Selected poems, 1938–1988* (Kimon Friar, Trans.). New York, NY: BOA Editions.

Rukeyser, Muriel. (1996). *The life of poetry*. Ashfield, MA: Paris Press.

Schneier, Lisa. (2001). Apprehending poetry. In Eleanor Duckworth (Ed.), *"Tell me more" listening to learners explain*. New York, NY: Teachers College Press.

Stern, Bert. (2009). *Steerage*. Somerville, MA: Ibbetson Street Press.

Tsur, Reuven. (2008). *Toward a theory of cognitive poetics*. Brighton: Sussex University Press.

PART 2

Biology

CHAPTER 3

Poetry in a Biology Classroom

Urszula Golebiewska

The use of poetry across the disciplines has gained momentum in the past decade. There are multiple case reports, examples, and materials available online, as well as several studies published in serious journals. In this chapter I am going to describe my experience using poems in my biology classes at Queensborough Community College. I will address my motivations, reflect on my assignments and collected student reflections, and conclude with the ways I am planning to modify my poetry assignments for the future. While my motivations to integrate poetry were genuinely based on a personal interest, I will also include a brief introduction and discussion of the benefits that poetic expression brings into the science education.

Many students register for biology classes thinking that it is one of the easier courses among science disciplines, but biology is a serious scientific subject and biology classes are rigorous. A large number of students are underprepared for the challenges of traditional lectures in the discipline, and many require additional resources and motivating assignments. Biology educators have developed multiple approaches to enhance students' experiences and learning; however, despite intensive efforts, the success rate in biology classes is not as high as expected (in some years only 35% of students achieve C or better in the first semester of General Biology).

One of the approaches investigated is incorporation of cross disciplinary assignments including poetry, as the use of poetry in the science classroom may engage and enhance students' understanding of abstract and complex concepts. This approach is particularly popular in K-12 levels, but it has also been explored at the university level. Unfortunately, there are not many reports describing the use of poetry in science classes in community colleges. The descriptive techniques that are shared by science and poetry allow for creative, critical, and metaphoric thinking, and they have the potential to capture the imagination of students at all educational levels and on all levels of academic preparedness.

1   Motivations: Personal and Professional

As stated, my interest in using poetry in a Biology Classroom is a selfish one or at least it stemmed from my personal love of poetry and of the particular way of expression that poetry offers. When thinking about projects for my students I thought first about the joy of sharing two things that I am passionate about: science and poetry. I used poetry in my classes because I thought it might be of similar interest to students, and that it might enrich their experience beyond the standard skills taught in the biology courses.

The link between poetry and science was shown to me early during my education. As a child I wrote poems in all my notebooks and was a member of poetry and poetry reciting clubs. I became a scientist partially because my physics teacher in junior high school told me, and managed to convince me, that physics is like poetry: both disciplines use a beautiful language, it's just the symbols that are different. In other words, poetry was my passion well before I learned that there are other things one could learn at school. Drawing an analogy between poetry and a scientific discipline that is usually seen as cold and accurate opened my eyes to other possibilities. In pushing my students towards different territories, I believe that I can enrich their experiences and open their eyes to other possibilities, as well.

In the past decade initiatives aimed at including arts into STEM education have ranged from using art in individual classes (Ainsworth, Prain & Tytler, 2011) to designing STEM curricula including art components.[1] In general, cross-disciplinary activities foster out-of-the-box thinking as they involve the use of discipline independent skills such as intuition and imagination. We are living in a world constantly transforming and gaining complexity and college education should prepare students for unforeseen challenges and problems. Teaching them to think outside the box will be beneficial in this regard.

While poetry is usually not directly associated with scientific disciplines, it includes the use of skills that are also important in science. In fact, because poems are a unique form of expression, they also provide a wonderful platform for very personal way to describe human emotions, experiences, and surrounding environment. These two factors—the need to bring biological concepts to students in a new way and the wonders of expression that poetry offers—has prompted many educators to include poetry in biology classes. There are numerous examples of the use of poems in biology classes at all levels, beginning with elementary schools and ending with medical schools. The benefits of poetry in medical education were mainly seen in increased levels of empathy and a deepened understanding of complex concepts (Wolters & Wijnen-Meijer, 2012; Pollack & Korol, 2013; Brown, 2015; Rankin & Brown, 2016). A very concise form of haiku was used in a neuroscience class to aid in understanding of neurodegenerative disorders. These assignments fostered logical thinking skills and seemed to improve empathy in the medical students.

These studies indicate that use of poetry in medicinal studies provide large scope learning benefits.[2]

At first I was very reluctant to include cross-disciplinary assignments in my classes as biology courses are content driven and very little room is allowed in traditional class for anything else. Additionally, biology is a challenging subject for the majority of students. It sounds deceptively easy and many students expect a breezy pass and are surprised to face this rigorous discipline like a head on gale hard to overcome. In the past I have tried multiple approaches to equip students with tools to combat these challenges, yet the difficulties posed for students by biology as a scientific discipline are multifaceted. First they have to acquire new technical vocabulary, then they have to acquire knowledge of basic laws of chemistry and physics. Next they have to employ concepts from chemistry and physics, and then they have to grasp abstract biological concepts. Additionally, there are units in their textbooks that require memorization, and students often get lost in the number of new words that form complex concepts.

Thankfully, Queensborough Community College promotes multiple initiatives to enhance teaching and learning experiences, and offers workshops to faculty to explore various ideas. During the Students Working in Interdisciplinary Groups (SWIG) workshop I felt envious of English Instructors who incorporated poems into their projects as I am a poetry enthusiast from an early age and miss it in my classrooms. As I often encourage students to break course concepts into smaller parts and to use analogies to bring scientific terms closer to their lives, I asked myself whether it was possible to incorporate poetry into biology classes. I concluded that poetry is a rich form of expression that can be used in teaching any subject.

My first experience using poetry with QCC biology students was a reflection written after their Service Learning project. My biology students took a class of 5th graders for a field trip. This particular section was also Writing Intensive and it the reflection was assigned as one of the low stakes assignments. At first students were confused but once I gave them a few examples they all enjoyed the experience. Another project that I implemented was a collaboration between English and Biology classes. The main idea was for students to read poems associated with ecology. Biology students were responsible for explaining the scientific terms encountered in the texts. In addition, I also used a poem as a part of a quiz in an Introduction to Biology for Science Majors (Bi 115) class. Students read the poem and were supposed to figure out which components of a cell each strophe the poem described. The descriptions were quite different from the standard textbook definitions. Finally, the most creative assignment that I gave students was writing a poem about one of their favorite microorganisms. In general, these assignments were geared to inspire imagination and thoughtfulness and to promote thinking outside the rigid forms of scientific expressions.

When asked, science students are usually not too excited about reading poetry; however, once they are exposed to it in an easy and playful way they have the tendency to open up. Poetry offers a different form of expression and may help students deepen the difficult concept. I found that reading poems in a science class is a productive way to help students see science in a new way and in everyday life and to make more personal connections to the subjects they study.

Paradox, creative thinking, attention to detail, discovery, and humor all can be found in a good poem and in a scientific inquiry problem. Thus, poetry can be used to instill skills that are necessary in a science class. Students often learn skills and concepts in isolation and have trouble to transfer acquired knowledge between different subjects bringing very different medium into the classroom might help foster cross discipline connections. It was suggested that such a transfer of concepts across domains is a powerful cognitive tool. The idea was investigated to certain degree particularly on the crossroads of medicine and poetry and the outcomes were positive.

2   Student Assignments and Reflections

Following is a description of the assignments that I used in my classes, as well as specifics on how I plan to modify them to provide enriched experiences in my future classes.

2.1   *Poetry as a Tool for Writing Reflections*

General Biology for majors is a cornerstone course that all biology majors have to complete prior to engaging in advanced courses. Therefore, it is important to prepare students for future studies in biology as well as giving them rounded overall education. Queensborough Community College offers a 200 level General Biology course that spans two semesters.

My second semester of General Biology for majors (Bi 202) was involved in a service learning project. The core part of the project was for my students to lead a class of 5th graders on a field trip around nearby pond called Oakland Lake. The assignment included collecting samples of leaves, acorns, branches and other plant material. Nest, back in the lab the collected samples were described and analyzed. My students helped the school children in filling worksheets describing leaves, seeds, acorns cones and winter branches and in identification of the tree species around the pond based on the samples collected. At the conclusion of their project students were required to write a reflection about their experience. The walk around the pond was challenging as the children and particularly boys were rather handful. My students were tired and had hard time concentrating. Writing a free form reflection was challenging for many of them and I decided to ask them to write a reflective poem. Post assignment reflections are often difficult for science students as they are accustomed to very structured forms such as laboratory reports. Providing sets of questions limits somewhat the scope and details that might have touched a student in unexpected ways. The students were shy about writing a poem at first but it turned out to be an easier task than writing a reflective essay at the end. Poems in general are shorter and more condensed. Students were concerned about rhymes, but once they realized that rhymes are not necessary and let their thoughts gather on the paper they were proud of their work and the project they just completed. The poem was very simple, consisting of descriptive phrases, but also very honest and warm. It started: "It was a nice day, the children came for the walk around the lake. We taught them about leaves." Writing the poem together brought the class closer. Through the reflection I also learned that students gained more from the experience than I expected. Here is an example of reflection: "This was more than a trip to learn about the leaves." Moreover, some students began asking: "Why did we lose the enthusiasm and curiosity in finding new things about the world?" This exercise taught me that low stake writing assignments can be tailored to more personal expression forms. In the future I would structure the assignment in more detail. Most of the students employed a free form to write their reflections and now I think that giving them more structural framework (for example a sonnet) to follow might be even more beneficial.

2.2   *Poetry as a Tool for a Quiz that Breaks Routine*

In general, most of written assignments in a science class test for content knowledge and students are accustomed to write research papers, laboratory reports or papers based on reading scientific literature. Such assignments often require understanding, applying, and analyzing facts and results. Assignments requiring high level of creativity or artistic imagination are rare. Moreover traditional assignments and tests might seem stifling and boring to students being exposed to science for the first time. One of the most challenging classes for me to teach was the Introduction to Biology for Science Majors (Bi 115). The class was designed to be a stepping stone into more rigorous General Biology class (Bi 201) but majority of students enrolled were non-science majors. Every lecture required new, interesting and effective assignments to engage students. During a lecture on cells I decided to use a poem describing intracellular structures to help students remember them better. The students were falling asleep while I showed them movies, animations and images the week before and I decided to replace typical quiz questions with a poem. I found the poem on one of the numerous websites with repositories of materials to implement poetry in biology classes. Each strophe of the poem described a different intracellular organelle without providing its name. It was filled with analogies and metaphors. The poems used references to "real life" situations with phrases: "I am like a traffic light," "My job is to be the grocery store," or "I am like a vending machine." The assignment was very simple: read a poem and identify which cellular parts are being described. At the end of the assignment I asked students to write a short reflection describing their personal opinions about this form of a test. In general students found the assignment more difficult than other types of quizzes and tests (their favorite were cross-word puzzles), but their comments were most encouraging. Here are some of them:

> I personally don't really like poems, however, I thought that this assignment was actually kind of interesting. I think we remember more with these kinds of assignments.

> It was a little difficult to come up with the right response because it is not using definitions but descriptions.

> I liked this poem because in each paragraph it gives a hint but it is kind of difficult to figure out [what] the key word is.

> I think it was confusing and a little fun because it really made us think.

> You forget you are taking a test when it is put in a fun way.

> I'm not used to reading poems related to science. I found it surprising. I look forward to another assignment like this.

For me reading these comments was like a breath of fresh air. Students attested that the assignment not only helped them learn but also gave them a fun way to learn science. Students themselves realized that poetry might help in the learning process.

I was very pleasantly surprised with my introductory class response to the poem as most students described the assignment as interesting and fun.

My fear was that they will see it as yet another attempt to make them work hard. Students also indicated that it was challenging to read descriptive and allegorical language rather than straight forward definitions. It indicates that they really engaged higher cognitive modes to make a link between metaphors and allegories and scientific terms. Some students express interest in more assignments involving reading poems and I am really happy about it. Some students admitted that they do not like reading poems but that they found assignment involving them nevertheless interesting. For some students it showed that one can write poetry about science, opening their eyes to other possibilities. I will definitely try it again.

The assignments broaden students' horizons on top of offering a challenging way of asking questions. Some students indicated that they never read poems related to science and some that they do not like reading poems at all, but through this assignment they were exposed to new experiences and found them interesting and engaging.

2.3   *Poetry as a Tool for Written Assignments*

Poetry enhances skills that are also important in science, for example imagination, analysis, observation, and clear communication. The transfer of skills between disciplines reinforces these skills. Active use of metaphors helps instill abstract concepts and employment of learners' imagination helps deconstruct and construct perception of science. Poetry can serve as a medium to link and distinguish observations and assumptions, and has potential to enrich learning. Some educators embrace arts and science as manifestations of the same human creativity. Thus it makes sense to entangle these two activities to enhance students' learning.

One of the more challenging chapters during the second semester of the majors General Biology course (BI 202) is the chapter about protists as this group of organisms is the most diverse among eukaryotes. Students have to learn about large number of unfamiliar organisms with complicated names and even more complicated life cycles. Most of the students do not perform well on tests about protists because they are overwhelmed with the amount of material. On a spur of the moment when students asked me for an extra credit assignment I told them to write a poem about their favorite protist or group of protists. This assignment allowed students to think deeper and to form closer and more personal relationship with the subject. First, students had to choose the organisms to write about and then describe it in a personal manner. Most of the students showed a deep understanding and thoughtfulness in their work. They showed connections and appreciations for the protists that they learned in class.

Some of the students' works showed use of protists to reference deeper existential issues: "Single cell, oh well, why can't life be this simple," and alluding to a stress-free life of an organisms reproducing asexually. Some students made playful statements about taking revenge on protists by eating sushi (that is wrapped with a protist, red algae). While some made deep existential comments about magnificent sharks being killed by red ties (caused by protists called dinoflagellates).

In summary I found this assignment to be very enriching both for students and for myself. I truly enjoyed reading the submitted poems. Students, in their work, showed good deal of understanding of protestant structures and life styles. In the past I used to ask students to write a regular essay about protists but in the future I will continue to ask students to write poems. Writing poetry pushed students towards more creative thoughts and deeper connections to the organisms they were writing about, and hopefully towards longer lasting memories about the class.

2.4 *Poetry as a Collaborative Assignment*

Paradox, creative thinking, attention to detail, discovery, and humor all can be found in a good poem and in a scientific inquiry problem. Thus, poetry can be used to instill skills that are necessary in a science class. Students often learn skills and concepts in isolation and have trouble to transfer acquired knowledge between different subjects. Bringing very different medium into the classroom might help foster cross discipline connections and life-long learning. It was suggested that such a transfer of concepts across domains is a powerful cognitive tool. The idea was investigated to certain degree particularly on the crossroads of medicine and poetry.

Students Working in Interdisciplinary Groups (SWIG) is one of the high impact practices used at Queensborough Community College. Literature can help to bring scientific topics into more life-relevant space which is very important as often students try to learn scientific topics in a vacuum and have difficulties seeing the necessity of using scientific knowledge on a regular basis. It seemed a natural step to include some poetry into my classes. With a colleague from the English Department we tried to implement a collaborative project involving reading poetry. The project had few steps; one of them was the introduction of new scientific vocabulary where biology students helped defining terms pertaining to ecology. The last stage of the project was an analysis of poems referring to ecology. This particular class was very science intense and less open to projects outside the box. I learned that students need both a certain degree of freedom when faced with open ended assignments as well as a set of very clear objectives. The assignment was centered on students in an English class reading poems about science instead of other poems; in the future I will reverse it more towards the biology students reading poems about science instead of a textbook. I would like to expand the project in the future to make students read more poems associated with ecology and analyze particular ecosystems described.

Ecology is the last topics in Bi 202, and towards the end of semester students are usually exhausted and need extra stimulation, unusual assignments involving poetry might be one of the options to spark their interest.

3   Concluding Thoughts

In summary my use of poetry in the classroom so far is not very extensive as I decided to include poems mainly out of personal interest. The Symposium, "Poetry Across the Curriculum," opened my eyes to instructors at QCC interested in use of poetry as well as to the published reports on the use of poetry across the country. There are a lot of educators exploring a light wait song-like poems for K-12 education level and that raised my interest in the use of poetry in my classes. However, reading reports from medical schools increased my drive towards the subject. A Community College student population is characterized by large diversity; in every class there are students at all levels of preparedness and with multiple interests and experiences. In such a diverse group unusual assignments have a great potential to have a deep impact. I will definitely expand the range of assignments in both major and non-major classes to include both reading and writing poems. I hope to show to my students that both science and poetry can have place in everybody's life. In addition, I found that poetry can help in many aspects of teaching and learning starting with new vocabulary acquisition and ending with a bit of humor to dissipate a challenging situation. My experience with positive outcomes of poetry in a science classroom encouraged me to use it more often.

Notes

1   For example, the State University of New York at Potsdam, supported by Lockheed Martin, developed a program that combines arts, humanities and STEM fields. The goal of the program is to educate young minds to solve complex problems facing humanity (Madden et al., 2013).
2   Several researchers identified benefits of use poetry in medical education. (Brown, 2015; Rankin & Brown, 2016; Wolters & Wijnen-Meijer, 2012).

References

Ainsworth, Shaaron, Prain, Vaughan, & Tytler, Russell. (2011). Drawing to learn in science. *Science, 333*(6046), 1096–1097.

Brown, Sherry-Ann. (2015). Creative expression of science through poetry and other media can enrich medical and science education. *Front Neurol, 6*, 3.

Madden, Margaret E., Baxter, Marsha, Beauchamp, Heather, Bouchard, Kimberley, Habermas, Derek, Huff, Mark, Ladd, Brian, Pearon, Jill, & Plague, Gordon. (2013). Rethinking STEM education: An interdisciplinary steam curriculum. *Procedia Computer Science, 20*, 541–546.

Pollack, Alexia E., & Korol, Donna L. (2013). The use of haiku to convey complex concepts in neuroscience. *Journal of Undergraduate Neuroscience Education, 12*(1), A42–A48.

Rankin, Jean, & Brown, Val. (2016, March). Creative teaching method as a learning strategy for student midwives: A qualitative study. *Nurse Eduction Today, 38*, 93–100.

Wolters, Frank J., & Marjo, Wijnen-Meijer. (2012). The role of poetry and prose in medical education: The pen as mighty as the scalpel? *Perspectives on Medical Education, 1*(1), 43–50.

PART 3

English

CHAPTER 4

An Initiation into Academic Discourse with Poetry

Susan Lago

1   Introduction

Community college students often approach general education courses with the attitude that they are courses that they must get through on their way to the "real" ones they will take in their declared majors. They are not expecting, nor desirous of, academically rigorous coursework that challenges their assumptions about the world and their place in it. There is an opportunity, therefore, for teachers to engage students in the more idealistic goals of the academy, to introduce them to discourse, argument, and to a deeper way of thinking that moves away from the binary, in other words, to "speak our language" (Bartholomae, 2002: 3). Academic writing, and the thinking aloud on the page that such writing engenders, is key to students' facility in that language. The Council of Writing Program Administrators NCTE National Writing Project has developed a list of qualities that are necessary components, not only for composition courses, but also for writing across the curriculum, "habits of mind" that include "curiosity, openness, and flexibility" (Council of Wrtiting Program Administrators, 5). In this chapter, I will discuss a poetry focused in-class activity that is an effective pedagogical strategy that introduces first and second-year students to concepts they will encounter in their academic journey, as well as to the rhetorical frameworks and "habits of mind" (Ibid.) necessary for academic success. Thus, an arts integrative curriculum that takes poetry out of the literature classroom and into disciplines not typically associated with the lyrical, the ephemeral, or the metaphoric, can help instructors create opportunities for students to have authentic conversations about challenging material.

2   Poetry across the Disciplines

Poetry encourages creative thinking across the disciplines, introduces language, and helps students connect their own feelings and experiences to the academic experience. In Clemson University's Poetry Project, Art Young, Patricia Connor-Greene, Jerry Waldvogel, and Catherine Paul found that "[w]hen poetry projects are well planned, they strengthen course goals" (Young et al., 2003: 16). For the Clemson University project, students wrote poetry that helped them interrogate complex, abstract concepts and put them into language comfortably within their own spheres of discourse. In particular, using poetry in such nonliterary disciplines as science or math, may actually reinforce course objectives and learning outcomes. Young et al. make the point that poetry is an "effective way to help students develop personal connections with science, because poetry allows them to step out of their traditional 'participant' role as science writers and adopt a more personalized 'spectator' role" (Ibid., 24). In other words, writing in non-disciplinary specific language allows students to make their own connections to the material, in effect, fostering the creative "habit of mind," recommended by the NCTE for success is postsecondary writing (Ibid., 1). Essentially, the integration of poetry into a nonliterary curriculum helps students learn how to learn.

Arts integration could, and should, start even before the student reaches college. For example, high school teacher John Kryder describes an integrative arts program at a Buffalo, New York high school where poetry is seen as an "inclusive art" that encourages interdisciplinary and collaborative discovery (Kryder, 2006: 34), or the "habit of mind" that is curiosity (Ibid., 1). He points out that poetry is "experiential," which means students experience it collectively as word and sound. He calls for pairings of humanities courses with STEM courses, with poetry acting as a catalyst for new ways of thinking about disciplinary concepts (Ibid., 35). For example, Rita Dove's poem, "Geometry," uses images of "windows, "hinges," and "butterflies" as metaphors for shapes, angles, and intersecting lines:

> I prove a theorem and the house expands:
> the windows jerk free to hover near the ceiling,
> the ceiling floats away with a sigh.
>
> As the walls clear themselves of everything
> but transparency, the scent of carnations
> leaves with them. I am out in the open
>
> And above the windows have hinged into butterflies,
> sunlight glinting where they've intersected.
> They are going to some point true and unproven. (Cited in ibid., 36)

Not only did the students in this class read and discuss poems about math, but they also wrote their own:

> On a good day,
> The hypotenuse stretches from A blue sailboat to Key West. On a bad day,
> Well, the numbers get ugly.
> Seems as though I'm traveling at a rate of x3m/s
> So before I'm only a point (h, k) In your viewing window
> I'll say goodbye. Goodbye.
> —Esther (Cited in Ibid.)

In using the metaphor of the sailboat to signify the angles of a triangle, this student more than rises to the occasion, as students are encouraged to do when asked to explore complex mathematical concepts through poetry (Ibid., 38).

For an arts integrated program such as Kryder's to be effective, the art part of it cannot just be a thematic overlay. Valuable class time devoted to the reading and writing of poetry is rewarded with surprising applications of discipline-specific vocabulary and engagement with core concepts, such as the application of mathematical principles to a problem involving shapes and lines. For example, in the Buffalo high school arts integrated program, student Dan wrote the following poem about the chemical compound, benzene:

> first a carousel of carbon flickered form to form
>   undetectable vibrations between shapes
> no norm but for some reason we still saw that
>   charcoal pit of doubt there was something
> about you no pencil could work out
> the rules told us four for carbon one for
>   hydrogen yet when we tried to use them to draw
> your skeleton you gave us neither strength nor
>   weakness not single and not double you
> were a shade we saw from inside our murky
>   little bubble
>
> the puzzle seemed so simple six C's and H's
>   right yet only now when we press our mind
> to you do you start to give us sight but
>   still we see your body as a smell and
>   though our
> nose it hooks structure structure a carousel is
>   only good for the chemistry books
> we know that you're alive in there we know
>   that you are breathing and if only we could

> see how that cloud you're in is seething how
> > the little ones run their races and take their
> > bows how your joints cannot be classified
> > how you fill all our hows
>
> —Dan (Cited in Ibid.)

The student plays with the words "carbon" and "hydrogen," recognizes the importance of "structure," and includes the chemical symbols "C" and "H." The student has become an agent of his own learning, taking ownership of knowledge acquisition through the language of metaphor and imagery. Margaret Freeman in her work on Cognitive Poetry states that the writers' creation of such metaphorical texts applies "the same analogical processes of reasoning that enable metaphor construction as the writers do who compose them" (Freeman, 2007: 1). Cognitive Poetics argues that it is "literature that is grounded in cognitive linguistic theory: namely, that literary texts are the products of cognizing minds and their interpretations the products of other cognizing minds," (Ibid.) which means that literary texts, such as poems, are a result of not only the writer's thinking, but also that the interpretation of those texts is the product of the reader's thinking mind. Thus, writer and reader make meaning together through "analogical mapping" (Ibid., 3). In the examples above from the Buffalo program, students and their classmates are mapping mathematical analogies together, acting as both writers and readers of each other's texts, reinforcing key concepts that may be lost or missed in the traditional lecture-quiz paradigm.

Unfortunately, the pressure on institutions of higher learning to churn out ready-to-work graduates results in arts programs getting short shrift, sometimes only showing up as core curriculum survey courses or electives. In 1999, Susan Koff saw a trend in undergraduate courses that lack true commitment from the university. She argues that a liberal "arts" education is comprised of a few core courses, which are decontextualized from social experience (Koff, 1999: 9–10). She suggests that if institutions designed curricula that took into account Howard Gardner's "ways of knowing," then "an integrative approach through intelligences would bring students to know *through* the arts" (Ibid., 12). The arts, then, are integral for undergraduate students who are learning how to learn. Koff asserts that poetry, with its surprising and ambiguous use of language and imagery, creates opportunities for students to move through "knowledge acquisition" to "knowledge synthesis" (Ibid.). Ultimately, these are the skills students will need in their working life (Ibid.). Addressing the concern that integrating arts into the curriculum will somehow distract from course content, Koff argues that the arts enhances that content rather than detracts from it (Ibid., 13). She claims that research shows that an arts integrated curriculum actually helps students "retain and recall … learning objectives" (Ibid.). In particular, the art of poetry, whether read, written and/or spoken, helps develop cognizing minds that are no longer simply passive receptacles waiting to be filled with teacher-knowledge (Freire, 2000: 12).

3   Learning to Learn

Humanities courses, and art curricula in particular, continue to be subjugated to the more marketable STEM academic pathways to a career. In her paper, "Poetry as Power: The Dynamics of Cognitive Poetics as a Scientific and Literary Paradigm," Margaret Freeman proposes an argument against overspecialization and the marginalization of the humanities, asserting that Cognitive Poetics provides an opportunity for understanding our world and our culture through the perceptions created by our senses (Freeman, 2005: 2). This approach is invaluable to interdisciplinary pedagogical practices. Arts integrated programs that treat learning as a holistic process recognize that students learn through multifaceted sensory learning styles, and that they are not only members of the university community, but also of their diverse cultural, socioeconomic, and gender identities. Sean Weibe et al. cite postmodern educator, D. Sawada, who raises the point that our teaching practices must consider that "the everyday student … does not leave life behind when entering school" (cited in Wiebe et al., 2007: 267). They bring their neighborhoods and families and friends with them into the uncharted territory of the academy. In her chapter on Cognitive Linguistic approaches to literary studies, Freeman claims that "[s]tudying … structuring metaphors provides a principled way to explain how writers are influenced by the metaphors of their culture while at the same time they are selecting and refining those metaphors to shape their own thinking and attitudes about the world around them" (Freeman, 2007: 8). In other words, literary metaphors are based upon the writer's cultural experience. She applies this claim to the understanding of literary texts, but it's not much of a stretch to see how Cognitive Poetics, or the study of human comprehension of making meaning through literary texts, can be applied across the disciplines. What would happen, for example, with integrating a psychology class, or philosophy, or neuroscience, with the study of poetry in this context? In such a pairing, art and science open up multiple ways of thinking, knowing, and learning, thus helping to foster students who are not afraid to pursue their own line of inquiry.

Academic inquiry does not exist in a vacuum, but rather arts, culture, and society exist on a rhizomatic continuum. Sean Wiebe et al. interrogate the opposite of root/tree hierarchy, the rhizome, which has no beginning or end. It is always middle. It seeks its own level. A rhizome represents multiplicity, something that is whole, yet, in the words of the poet Walt Whitman (1819–1892), "contain[s] multitudes" (Whitman, 1892). Wiebe et al. (2007: 267) argue for a truly integrated "embodied" curriculum that embraces disruption, flexibility, surprise, and diversity. Such an integrated curriculum must go beyond a surface thematic connection to a more comfortable interface. Wiebe calls for a rhizomatic approach to curriculum integration, one that is multitudinous and connective, one that allows for diametric thinking (Ibid., 264). The "a/r/tography" instructor is one who is a combination of, as Wiebe explains, *a*rtist, *r*esearcher, and *t*eacher. This concept makes possible arts integrative activities that arise from a living, dynamic classroom that embodies inquiry (Ibid., 265). Teaching and learning take place in the uncomfortable middle, a place that recognizes the value of surprise and failure (Ibid., 266). Rhizomatic pedagogy is nonlinear, nonhierarchical, and messy. It allows for "individual contextualized learning" through an inquiry-based arts integrated program (Ibid., 268). This living practice also recognizes students as a/r/tophophers and teaches them "how to sustain life-long learning ... through self-motivation (Ibid., 269). The a/r/tographer type of teacher is a "reflexive practitioner" (Ibid.). By engaging with "poiesis, the artful praxis of integration" teachers develop a living, breathing learning space that is part of a complex, ever-changing world (Ibid., 275). In such a program, poetry becomes a way of synthesizing knowledge through metaphor, community, and experience.

4   Classroom Practice

At Queensborough Community College, students are required to take English Composition I, an introductory writing course that teaches the basics of academic writing. In this course, a version of which is required at most two and four-year institutions, students must write essays that engage primarily with nonfiction texts. They read essays, newspaper articles, and narratives written by professional writers (for want of a better term). They may encounter ideas from Marx, Aristotle, bell hooks, Malcom Gladwell, and Susan Faludi. They read (or don't read), and come to class prepared to discuss the material. Except that, as first-year writers, students are unfamiliar, and uncomfortable, with "the discourse of our community" (Bartholomae, 2002: 3), in the words of David Bartholomae. In this new context, they struggle to make meaning, to bridge the gap between their own experiences and the language of the academy. Students may feel frustrated by their lack of understanding and may, as a result, resist these new ideas. They don't "get it." Kirk Kidwell, in his article "Understanding the College First-Year Experience," outlines four phases in the first-year experience: "dualism, multiplicity, relativism, and commitment in relativism" (Kidwell, 2005: 254). He identifies first-year college students fresh out of high school as dualistic thinkers who tend to see the world as either black or white (Ibid.). The students in the Clemson University project, suggests Catherine Paul of her art appreciation class, are often "intimidated" by high art and so turn away from immersing themselves in the experience and of trusting their own responses or the questions raised by the artwork they are viewing (Young et al., 2003: 35). Likewise Queensborough Community College's Composition students may resist difficult material by failing to develop the "habit of mind" that is engagement (Ibid.) with the material, except at a cursory level, and sometimes not at all.

As students transition from high school to college, they must discover new means of navigating unfamiliar territory that nevertheless has many of the hallmarks of the world so recently left behind. Kidwell understands that first-year college students must first overcome the challenges of managing their academic workloads and that in order to learn, they must become agents in their own academic experience. They have transitioned from high school, where they were containers who have been filled with information, to college students who are "active participants in the construction of knowledge" (Kidwell, 2005: 254). As Liane Robertson, Kara Taczak, and Kathleen Blake Yancey (2012) found in their research on students' abilities to successfully transfer writing skill sets grounded in prior knowledge, students are less likely to be successful when that knowledge fails to apply in a new academic setting. They may skim an assigned reading or else fail to read it at all, waiting instead for the teacher to explain it to them, or, in other words, to tell them what the text means. They are accustomed to learning from "the top down" (Shor, 2009: 282), as Ira Shor writes in his work on critical literacy. As they then move from dualistic thinking to relativism, where they see truth as being opinion, students try to game the system by telling professors what they think they want to hear (Kidwell, 2005: 254). Thus, when confronted with a question about their own interpretation, students try to answer with a guess as to what the professor thinks so they can fall into their more comfortable teaching-learning pattern.

One strategy for helping students make this transition, is a well scaffolded in-class poetry activity that can help them make meaning of difficult texts. For example, at Queensborough Community College, on the first day of class, I give my English Composition I students a handout of the poem, "My Papa's Waltz" by Theodore Roethke (Roethke, 1942):

> The whiskey on your breath
> Could make a small boy dizzy;
> But I hung on like death:
> Such waltzing was not easy.
>
> We romped until the pans
> Slid from the kitchen shelf;
> My mother's countenance
> Could not unfrown itself.
>
> The hand that held my wrist
> Was battered on one knuckle;
> At every step you missed
> My right ear scraped a buckle.
>
> You beat time on my head
> With a palm caked hard by dirt,
> Then waltzed me off to bed
> Still clinging to your shirt.

I instruct the class to read the poem to themselves. Next, they read the poem aloud, each student reciting a line or two until nearly every student has had a chance. I then ask students to read the poem again, this time noting words or images that caught their attention, and then yet another time, noting places of tension or ambiguity within the text. I urge them to take out their phones and look up the meanings of words they don't know and to write down those definitions.

In this exercise, students are performing academic tasks that are quite possibly new to them. They have now read the text, not once, but at this point, at least three times. They are practicing, as Robertson et al. write, the skills they will need to successfully apply their prior knowledge to new rhetorical situations (Robertson et al., 2012). In the next part of the in-class activity, students are tasked with writing down what they think the poem is about, and then finally, what they think the poem means. At this point, they have read the poem, heard the poem, and annotated it. They are reading as writers. Indeed, as Maria Salvatori writes in "The 'Argument of Reading' in the Teaching of Composition," when we teach reading, we teach students to create reflexive opportunities for knowledge (Salvatori, 2002). In other words, we are teaching them to read as interrogators of a text rather than as passive surveyors of it. We ask them to read for the purpose of being able to write critically in a new context.

Next, I separate the class into small groups, of no more than four students, that are tasked with coming to a consensus regarding their interpretation of Roethke's poem. I instruct them to share their evidence within the group, the evidence being the words and images they annotated, and to assign one student to take notes for the group. Now the conversation about the text is peer-to-peer. The teacher has stepped back and allowed discovery to unfold, as Ira Shor terms it, so that the students may share their subjective experiences to help each other, and themselves, to "make sense of the world and [their] place in it" (Shor, 2009: 282). This is crucial to the development of "critical literacy … that questions the social construction of the self" (Ibid.). Through sharing their interpretations and experiences, students now have the opportunity to step out of familiar territory made up of digital social networks and family, and take on new roles as scholars. Furthermore, students are able to find their way into the text using the language of the poem and their own interpretations of it while at the same time hearing and responding to the ideas of others. In the article, "Leading Initiatives for Integrative Learning," Mary Taylor Huber et al. discuss the importance of making such connections. When groups of students focus their attentions on common ideas and tasks, they are able to process a rapidly changing world, one that encompasses divergent points-of-view (Huber, 2007). Andrew Elfenbein in his article, "Cognitive Science and the History of Reading," finds that readers in different discourse communities bring their own skill sets and prior knowledge to the reading of a text, which results in different experiences of that text (Elfenbein, 2006: 486). Readers thus form concepts stemming from their own background knowledge, allowing them to make associations (Ibid., 489). They understand concepts through "cohort activation," a process by which readers make connections between the text they are reading and other texts, and/or their own personal experiences (Ibid.). Sharing their reading impressions in a group activity invites students to become part of a new discourse community. They are in the process of developing the "habit of mind" of openness to new ideas.

The group work facilitates student-centered problem solving as students work together examining and evaluating evidence. Typically, students are divided into two opinions about "My Papa's Waltz": one, that the "papa" in the poem is abusing a child; and the other, that a father and child are dancing around the room in a roughhousing fashion. This divergence of opinion gives students an opportunity to argue for their primacy of their interpretation. Etienne Wenger argues that we make meaning through social interactions and that this practice takes place in a variety of "communities of practice" (Wegner, 1988: 4, 6, 86, 102, 134, 136–137). On the first day of class, most first-year writing students are entering a new "community of practice," one that resembles the one from which they just came, but has a new set of rules and expectations. In short, they are learning the ways of their new community by making meaning together. In their work on integrative learning, Huber et al. identify the challenge of helping students "tie things together" (Huber, 2007), of helping them make connections between disparate ideas and arguments. Where else, she asks, "are students encouraged to make links among their academic, personal, and community lives?" (Ibid.). As an example, in this poetry-focused classroom activity, one student may recount to the group her personal history of family alcohol abuse to support her interpretation that the "papa" in the poem is an abusive alcoholic, pointing out the words "whiskey," "scrape" and "beat" (Roethke, 1942). Another may remember reading the poem in high school and asserts his former English teacher's interpretation as the "correct" one, and yet another shares a memory of dancing on her father's feet as her interpretation of the lines: "But I hung on like death/Such waltzing was not easy" (Ibid.). Thus, to answer Huber's question, the community college classroom is the place where students start making those connections between the personal and the academic, and between the academic and their new interactional "community of practice" (Wenger, 1998).

This student-led conversation lends itself to active discussion that works across the disciplines. For example, a psychology class might look at the poem through the lens of Theodore Roethke's mental illness (Dorset, 2005: 455), or a class in social work might discuss the poem in the context of child abuse. Nursing students might use the text as a launching point for a discussion about alcoholism, and a biology class, the genetic predisposition toward the affliction. Young claims that poetry is a means to get students to write not within the discipline of nursing, for example, or even to write across the disciplines of literature and nursing, but to actually use poetry to subversively write against the curriculum (Young, 2003: 474). When a student makes a connection between his own experience with alcoholism to the lines, "The whiskey on your breath/Could make a small boy dizzy" (Roethke, 1942), and then to a particular scientific concept having to do with the body's mechanism for metabolizing alcohol, then that student has learned to think about science in all its societal and human implications. Young et al. examine Clemson University's experience with using poetry in such a biology class. When Jerry Waldvogel asked his students to make a connection between the following poem about the scientific process by J. Brooks Knight and everyday scientists' philosophy toward their work: "Say not that this is so,/but that this is how it seems to me to be/as I now see the things I think I see" (Young et al., 2003: 25). One of his students responded by writing a poem instead of an essay:

> The goal of good science is to understand
> Nature, the universe, the law of the land.
> But science has certain rules by which one must abide
> So the results gained are truly justified,
> And on its own the outcome can clearly stand.
>
> The behaviors we see once are not always true,
> For reliability we must observe other examples too.
> True science depends on validation,
> A quality achieved by replication,
> So we must test a hundred times, not just a few.
>
> This is why we cannot just say "this is so,"
> After a million times we still do not know.
> For science is not in the market to prove,
> It wants only that which is false to remove,
> And allow valid ideas the room to grow. (Cited in Ibid.)

What surprised Waldvogel was how well the student had understood the scientific process (Ibid.). Likewise, a student arguing that her own experience shines a light on the question of whether or not the father in "My Papa's Waltz" abuses alcohol, is making a personal connection to the text, one that can be used to posit a claim that can then be supported with textual evidence. Further, reading the text and discussing it with her peers has given this student a model for how to think about one's own thinking, as well as the poet's thinking, and the thinking of one's peers. Thus, the student's own thinking is "ignited by the thoughts of others," which, according to Salvatori, makes necessary the activity of reading, not as an excuse to have students write, but as the "context for writing" (Salvatori, 2002: 352). Reading poetry, then, becomes the context through which disciplinary goals may be achieved.

After about ten minutes, I ask students to select one of their group to present their findings to the class. They quickly huddle together, making decisions about who will speak and what they will share. Another layer has been added to the activity, one that requires students to express themselves verbally to share their response to accomplish the specific task of articulating the collaborative interpretation of the poem (General Education (Pathways), QCC). Used as an in-class assignment, this kind of poetry activity also has the benefit of drawing out the quiet, more reserved student (Young et al., 2003: 15) who may hesitate to volunteer in front of the entire class. This student may choose to be the note taker instead of the presenter, for example, or may share within the peer-only confines of the group. They contribute in some way. Through poetry, these quieter students gain the confidence to lend their voices to the class discussion.

Poetry can also broaden and enhance students' language use as they become comfortable with expressing their own ideas and values in relation to poetry. As students present to the class, I reflect back to them what they've said, picking up on key ideas and motifs, but being careful not to appropriate the student's response or to "correct" it. I ask open-ended questions, such as, "Is it possible to be drunk without being an alcoholic?" As John Montague points out in his article detailing his correspondence with Roethke in 1960, the poet's father was "a strict German" (Montague, 1996: 561), but not a drunk. When offered this biographical information, the strict German father who worked in a greenhouse (Ibid.), students revisit to the line, "You beat time on my head/ With a palm caked hard by dirt" (Roethke, 1942), and focus instead on the work-hardened hand rather than the word "beat." Students are now focusing on specific language: What does it mean to be drunk? To be an alcoholic? What are some other meanings of the word beat? Can a word mean two things at the same time? Young et al. found that this reflective exchange, where poetry is the catalyst, strengthens the bond between teacher and student and fosters communication (Young et al., 2003: 15). In his discussion on critical literacy, Ira Shor notes that "monolithic discourse that sets the agenda from the top down is dialogic discourse" that must in turn give way to a more bottom up approach (Shor, 2009). Such a "bottom up" activity makes possible interdisciplinary discourse, which is especially important in courses that tend towards "monolithic" means of communicating course material. When teachers create opportunities for students to engage in reflexive critical dialogue with texts, students become active, not passive, learners (Salvatori, 2002: 358). Students thus become agents of their own learning; they display "persistence," or the "habit of mind" (Ibid., 1) that has allowed them to work through the text to discovery of meaning.

When all the groups have presented, I ask students to individually write a paragraph about their own interpretation of the poem. They should take into consideration their group discussion as well as their own annotations of the poem. For some first-year writers, the direction to write about their own ideas is in direct opposition to what they've been taught, mainly to summarize or to restate someone else's ideas (oftentimes the teacher's). In their book on writing across contexts, Yancey et al. recount a case study involving a student, "Emma." This student found that the strategies she had learned in high school, which were to write a relatively error-free paper that reflected perfectly the instructor's expectations, led her to be replicate her high school success in her first-year writing courses. When moving beyond these courses, however,

Emma found that her skills, namely correct grammar and pleasing the teacher, were not sufficient in new writing contexts. In essence, she held onto behaviors, but didn't develop the necessary grounding in reflection and theorizing she would need to transfer her skills to new writing situations (Yancey, Robertson & Taczak, 2014: 66–82). Likewise, the Composition I students in my class often volunteer that correct grammar is the hallmark of good writing, some sadly remembering their high school papers handed back all marked up in red. Poetry, which eschews rigid sentence structures, offers them a way into language that is playful, ambiguous, or sensory; punctuation may or may not be present. In the Clemson University Poetry Project, Young et al. conclude that poetry offers a way of allowing students to use poetic language to understand complicated ideas without them having to be familiar with "what to them is an alien discourse" (Young et al., 2003: 41). For my students, their individual paragraphs are their foray into this discourse. While most of them echo what the majority of students thought about the poem, they've still made a first step into writing their way to understanding the text. What's interesting is that typically, the majority carries the interpretation that finds its way into these individual paragraphs. When the majority of the class argues that the poem is about an abusive alcoholic, so go the paragraphs. A rare class aligns itself with the view that "My Papa's Waltz" is a father-son dance, a literal "waltz." When they do, however, the paragraphs reflect this majority view. Few students, if any, complicate their views by theorizing that the poem is, as Montague writes in his discussion of the poet's work, "dense with physical memories of the soiling of childhood, full of little comforting cries and invocations against the dark powers" (Montague, 1996: 2). For them, the poem is either this or that. That they've internalized their classmates' views in this early venture is fine, however. Appropriation is, as Bartholmae argues, somewhere between the student's "primary discourse" and the new academic one they are just now encountering (Bartholomae, 2002: 13). They've entered the conversation. They read the poem and came away thinking one thing and ended up thinking another. They've moved from Kidwell's dualistic thinking to something more approximating the "commitment in relativism" (Kidwell, 2005: 254) of their future academic selves. They've learned that positions must be supported by evidence and to consider counterarguments (Ibid.). This poetry exercise gives them practice in engaging with others' positions, moving beyond opinion (I liked it/understood it) to reason-based arguments supported by textual evidence. As they grow into becoming critical thinkers, these first-year students will eventually learn that there is no one "right" answer, not an absolute, professor-blessed truth that will earn them an A, and that in fact, often their questions will be countered with other questions (Ibid., 255).

Finally, individual students each write one final paragraph where they describe something new that they learned. This could be about the poem, poetry, themselves, or something else. This metacognitive stage, where they reflect upon their own learning, is the capstone of the activity. One of The Council of Writing Program Administrators NCTE National Writing Project's qualities necessary for academic success in college is the ability to write about one's own thinking. The metacognitive task, they claim, encourages students to consider multidisciplinary contexts, asks them to view their own writing as texts, and helps them to make connections about the choices they've made in terms of audience and purpose (Council of Writing Program Administrators). In my first-day of class exercise, students are not yet familiar with such an activity, but it's a first step. In their paragraphs, some students describe information they learned about Theodore Roethke, others about taking notes or looking up words. Some students, however, write about how they were able to change their thinking, either about poetry in general, or "My Papa's Waltz" in particular. The NCTE study finds that such opportunities for reflection prepare students to apply skills learned on one project to future writing projects (Ibid.). As they read their reflections aloud, students engage with their audience, their teacher and classmates, and by extension, the larger academic community. They've flexed some new muscles, displayed curiosity, openness and flexibility, other "habits of mind," which the NCTE finds are crucial to student success beyond first-year courses (Ibid., 2–4).

5   Conclusion

In less than two hours, students have written for a sustained period on three separate occasions. They've written about a text, about their ideas about the text, and about their thinking about reading, writing, and learning. They've articulated arguments using textual evidence as support to their peers and they've collaborated with those peers to deepen their analysis of the text. Students made choices about which ideas are stronger than others, who will take notes for the group, and who will present the group's findings to the class. The teacher has facilitated a class discussion, helping students make connections between the poem and course outcomes. After close reading, annotation, and discussion, they are now ready to compose a paragraph advancing their own argument. Finally, students have distilled and clarified for themselves what they have learned. This activity can be used across the curriculum to introduce students to key disciplinary concepts. In the Humanities as well as the STEM disciplines, poetry is a way to help students develop the habits of mind they will need to become scholars in the true sense. Thus, such first-year experiences that integrate reading, writing, and critical thinking skills, help students adapt to new rhetorical situations, and facilitate their ability to transfer these processes across "multiple environments."[1] In particular, poetry teaches students that academic inquiry involves multiple layers and methods in arriving at understanding. Furthermore, poetry opens up not only the students' thinking, but the teacher's as well as we work with students to make connections. For example, I learn what they don't understand about the poem conceptually and words they don't know, or I get a glimpse into their personal lives. Moreover, every time I teach the poem, I learn something new about it. This insight is something I share with my students, that a reader can recursively return to a text again and again and each time discover new meaning.

Note

1 Ibid.

References

Bartholomae, David. (2002). Inventing the university. In T. R. Johnson (Ed.), *Teaching composition: Background readings* (3rd ed., pp. 2–30). Boston, MA: Bedford/St. Martin's.
Dorset, Phyllis F. (2017). Roethke remembered. *Sewanee Review, 113*(3), 450–458.
Elfenbein, Andrew. (2006). Cognitive science and the history of reading. *PMLA, 121*(2), 484–502.
Freeman, Margaret H. (2005). Poetry as power: The dynamics of cognitive poetics as a scientific and literary paradigm. In Harri Veivo, Bo Pettersson, & Merja Polvinen (Eds.), *Cognition and literary interpretation in practice* (pp. 31–57). Helsinki: Helsinki University Press. Retrieved from https://ssrn.com/abstract=1427831
Freeman, Margaret H. (2007). Cognitive linguistic approaches to literary studies: State of the art in cognitive poetics. In Dirk Geeraerts & Hubert Cuyckens (Eds.), *The Oxford handbook of cognitive linguistics* (pp. 170–187). New York, NY: Oxford University Press.
Freire, Paulo. (2000). *Pedagogy of the oppressed* (30th ed.). New York, NY: Continuum.
General Education (Pathways). (2017). *Queensborough community college*. Retrieved February 26, 2017, from http://www.qcc.cuny.edu/gened/index.html
Huber, Mary Taylor, Hutchings, Pat, Gale, Richard, Miller, Ross, & Breen, Molly. (2007). Leading initiatives for integrative learning. *Liberal Education, 93*(2), 46–51. Retrieved from https://www.aacu.org/publications-research/periodicals/leading-initiatives-integrative-learning

Johnson, Kristine. (2013). Beyond standards: Disciplinary and national perspectives on habits of mind. *College Composition and Communication, 64*(3), 517–541.

Kidwell, Kirk S. (2005). Understanding the college first-year experience. *Clearing House: A Journal of Educational Strategies, Issues and Ideas, 78*(6), 253.

Koff, Susan R. (1999). The role of the arts in undergraduate. *The Journal of General Education, 48*(1), 9–16.

Kryder, John B. (2006). Discovering the inclusive art of poetry. *The English Journal, 96*(1), 34–39.

Montague, John. (1996). Gentle giant. *Southern Review, 113*(3), 450–457.

Robertson, Liane, Tacsak, Kara, & Blake Yancey, Kathleen. (2012). Notes toward a theory of prior knowledge and its role in college composers' transfer of knowledge and practice. *Composition Forum, 26*, 1–21.

Roethke, Theodore. (1942). *My Papa's Waltz PoetryFoundation.org*. Retrieved from https://www.poetryfoundation.org/poems-and-poets/poems/detail/43330

Salvatori, Maria. (2002). The 'argument of reading' in the teaching of composition. In Timothy Barnett (Ed.), *Teaching argument in the composition course: Background readings* (pp. 346–361). Boston, MA: Bedford/St. Martin's.

Shor, Ira. (2009). What is critical literacy? In R. D. Torres, A. Darder, & M. P. Baltodano (Eds.), *The critical pedagogy reader* (pp. 282–297). New York, NY: Routledge. Retrieved from http://newlearningonline.com/literacies/chapter-7/shor-on-critical-literacy

Wenger, Etienne. (1998). *Communities of practice: Learning, meaning and identity*. Cambridge: Cambridge University Press.

Whitman, W. (2016). *Leaves of grass: The original 1855 edition*. Lavergne, TN: Value Classic Reprints.

Wiebe, Sean, Sameshima, Pauline, Irwin, Rita, Leggo, Carl, Gouzouasis, Peter, & Grauer, Kit. (2007). Re-imagining arts integration: Rhizomatic relations of the everyday. *The Journal of Educational Thought (JET)/Revue De La Pensée Éducative, 41*(3), 263–280. Retrieved from http://www.jstor.org.qbcc.ezproxy.cuny.edu:2048/stable/23765522

Yancey, Kathleen Blake, Robertson, Liane, & Taczak, Kara. (2014). *Writing across contexts: Transfer, composition, and sites of writing*. Logan, UT: Utah University Press.

Young, Art, Connor-Greene, Patricia, Waldvogel, Jerry, & Paul, Catherine. (2003). Poetry across the curriculum: Four disciplinary perspectives. *Language & Learning Across the Disciplines, 6*(2), 14–44.

Young, Art. (2003). Writing across and against the curriculum. *College Composition and Communication, 54*(3), 472–485.

CHAPTER 5

Poetry and Student Learning

Angela Hooks

> For what is a poem but a hazardous attempt at self-understanding: it is the deepest part of autobiography.
> ROBERT PENN WARREN, "Poetry is a kind of unconscious autobiography,"
> *New York Times*

∴

Identity, social and personal, is a motif that threads through my first-year college writing course. I use poetry and films to help student write about identity and how they affect and are affected by social, political and ethical matters. For first-year writing students, understanding identity in a social context based on culture, ethnicity, race, family, and faith illustrates they are not in isolation and that "good writing means telling the truth" (Lamott, 1994: 3) and that truth should "provoke and disturb" (Brown, 2014: 324) their audience. However, first-year writing students cringe when it comes to writing, and some have a disdain for poetry. I have discovered it's not the writing that causes students to cringe; it's the topic. Accustomed to teachers telling them what to write, they complain about boring topics, and uninteresting subjects. In an effort to curb that type of student attitude, I let students decide their subject and topic—a specific issue about a subject—whether the assignment is the autobiographical narrative, poetry collection, or the I-search paper. This method has become my standard agenda when teaching introductory composition courses at Dutchess Community College for Introduction to Composition, at The Culinary Institute of America for College Writing and at St. John's University for First Year Writing: Introduction to Composition.

In addition to a scholarly, academic approach to writing, I encourage students to write about their passion, something they will enjoy thinking, writing, reading, and researching for several weeks, and to explore the topic from multiple perspectives and rhetorical contexts. When students have a personal connection to the topic, they become active participants in the narrative and the research in which the topic becomes a specific issue about a subject. For example, a student chose the psychology of grief as a topic. He focused on personal and emotional problems and difficulties people faced with grief. He explored the effect grief had on identity. Thus, each writing assignments connected to the student's topic. For example, the student's poetry collection was about how he dealt with the grief of losing his father to cancer, and several classmates to suicide. His I-Search paper focused on how different people handled grief. During our fourteen-week semester the student had a personal connection with his topic. Therefore, the student became an active participant in the narrative and in the research imagining a scene "composed of people engaged in culturally recognizable activities with which the ideas being talked about have meaning" (Tannen, 2017: 361). Thus the topic for that student was not boring.

Many first-year writing students also cringe when it comes to writing poetry. However, I use poetry to show students poetry is a narrative, another way to tell a story. Sometimes parts of their poems become part of their autobiographical essay or even their I-Search paper. Other times writing a poem helps the student see their topic from a new perspective. The technique used is imitative poetry. During the poetry workshop unit, each student deals with the same poetry form, structure, and subject matter, which makes the students more attentive and interactive in class. Poet Mary Oliver concurs, claiming "each writer becomes interested in and learns from the work of the other members" (Oliver, 1994: 4).

This chapter discusses three poetry-writing assignments and three films used to teach first-year writing students how to use poetry as narrative and as autobiographical writing. Imitative poetry allows students to imitate the style and theme of a poem or directly talk back to the poet. Imitating is an exercise in mimicking the rhythm, language, style or subject of another poem. Mimicry and plagiarism are not the same. When a poet mimics, another poet has influenced her work; when a poet plagiarizes, she has stolen someone's style claiming it as her own without citing or giving credit (Dierking, 2002: 7–10). The purpose of mimicking allows the student to consider elements such as a narrator, imagery, structure—beginning, middle, and end—figurative language, conflict, tone and sound all combined to create a noteworthy narrative. Done often enough, the student might be able to incorporate a specific trait admired by a poet.

Moreover, a beginning student would learn very little if they were not allowed to imitate. Thus, transcendentalist Walt Whitman (1819–1892) influenced Allen Ginsberg (1926–1997) and Langston Hughes (1902–1967). Gwendolyn Brooks (1917–2000) influenced Terence Hayes. Robert Lowell (1917–1977) influenced Sylvia Plath (1932–1963) and Anne Sexton (1928–1974). Paul Laurence Dunbar (1872–1906) influenced Maya Angelou. In class, we look at Ginsberg's poem *Howl* influenced by Whitman's "Song of Myself," and Hayes' "Golden Shovel" influenced by Brooks' "We Real Cool." Written one hundred years apart both Paul Laurence Dunbar's "Sympathy" and Maya Angelou's "Caged Bird" poems mirror each other in subject matter. These poets read other poets and practiced imitation until they found a voice and story of their own. Yet, before writing poems students should start with their own ideas and thoughts. As Brooks said in an interview she does not think about what others have wrote—their form or structure; instead she starts with an idea or a thought. This points to the importance of students choosing a topic when they begin to write.

Talking back to the poet does not require the student to understand the poem in any "complete or even meaningful sense yet the student should discover something meaningful, interesting or insightful about the poem. Therefore, the "new poem reiterates the original poem" (Alderson, 1996). One semester, we read Jamaica Kincaid's short story *Girl* (Kincaid, 1978). *Girl* speaks to identity based on culture and gender. Although not a poem, the 650-word story has elements of a poem—chosen sound, imagery, structure and meaning, as well as language and diction.

Girl offended one student. As a result, the student answered *Girl* back, explaining that a girl is more than domestic help, and that she does not have to be prim and proper. Even though the student missed the social and political implications of the story, and she cared little about the structure of the story she pushed back against stereotypically gendered roles for girls, proving that women are more than domestic beings and their sexuality should not deem them "slut" material.

Such writing assignments challenge first-year writing students to understand identity in a social context based on culture, ethnicity, race, family, and faith illustrating they're not in isolation. They also indicate how "good writing means telling truth" that provokes and disturbs (Brown, 2014: 324), just as the student portrayed in her talk back piece to Kincaid's *Girl.*

Poetry assignments show students how to write with rhythm, clarity, and conciseness. Rhythm comes with rewording and revision, and varying sentence length as a result the language should resemble human speech. Thus, poetic lines that are shortened or lengthened help the writer slow down or speed up, and then clarity takes place. The poem teaches the student to deliberately choose words that illustrate the senses, and create vivid imagery. In turn clarity should produce conciseness, teaching students to cut verbiage and be precise.

1   Films and Poetry

As an introduction to poetry, I have taught the films *Dead Poets Society* (1989) and *Love Jones* (1997) and *Howl* (2010). Only one film is shown during a three-week poetry workshop unit. *Dead Poets Society* has always been my favored film to discuss despite class size, gender and diversity. *Dead Poets Society* takes place in an all boy school and fits well when teaching at the Culinary Institute of America because most classes are predominately male students with one or two female students. However, one semester my nineteen culinary students were Black American, Asian, Asian American, Hispanic, White and East Indian. And for the first time there were six or seven female students. *Love Jones* fit perfectly in this classroom setting just as it did at St. John's University and Dutchess Community College. Each film portrays poetry in motion, poetry as part of a narrative, poetry as narrative, and poetry definitions.

The film *Howl* is about Allen Ginsberg's poem *Howl*. The film evokes the birth of a hipster as the new age; an identity Ginsberg wanted to mirror "angel-headed hipster" (Ginsberg, 1956: 9). However, the film reveals Ginsberg also wanted to hide his identity as a homosexual, one reason he didn't want his poem published. The poem *Howl* is a command and a confession of the poet's faith. In 112 paragraph-like lines, he rants and raves regarding his friends, politics, and social expectations. Animated passages in the film based on the poem demonstrate how words can have a striking imagery that visuals are more effective than the actual words. For example, in the poem Ginsberg compares war, capitalism and mainstream culture to the idolatrous god "Moloch." In the film, a skyscraper morphs into a gigantic bull engulfed in a fire stomping through city streets. People toss their babies into the fire symbolizing a sacrifice and soldiers march through the streets symbolizing war. Through the film and the poem, the student learns the importance of description and metaphor.

Ginsberg penned words and phrases in the poem that society deemed obscene. Hence, the poem was put on trial for its obscene content in 1956. The obscenity trial is part of the film and exemplifies freedom of speech. Thus, the student can think about language how to use words with varied meaning. For example, the prosecutor points to the words "blew" and "blown" (Ibid., 13) as crude, however, the linguistic professor on the witness stand claims the words can signify being tossed around by the wind as well as a sexual act. As Richard Hugo argues in *The Triggering Town*, "the subject should serve the words" sometimes "violating the facts" (Hugo, 1979: 5–6). Students learn when writing they owe more to the truth than reality because reality is subject to interpretation.

Sometimes students writing can become dull when writing about the same topic usually they are writing what they think the teacher wants to hear. Teaching Ginsberg's *Howl* both the poem and the film generates new ideas and perspectives about the student's topic. Imitating *Howl* triggers the imagination teaching students that they do not have a social or moral obligation to feel a certain way and they can write beyond what they think the teacher wants to read. As a result, the student's language should have details that correspond to their attitude toward the world and himself. Imitating *Howl*'s words and phrases teaches students how to reference people, places, ideas, and events. First, the student writer references something autobiographical that causes them to howl, to mourn, to laugh, or even rejoice about their topic. Then something mythical, like Ginsberg's "Moloch." And finally, they write phrases that illustrate rebellion against societal expectations. As a result, the student has written what looks like an unorganized poem but is a prolonged riff about their topic. They move from personal experience, to researching a mythical being that is a metaphor for their topic and then describing how not to conform to societal expectations.

In contrast *Love Jones* is a coming-of-age love story. The characters use poetry to speak to each other, and poetry becomes a conversation. One character defines poetry as "the possibility of language," while another tells his friends, he does not "need poetry to get a woman." The poetry in the film goes on to define love or rather make a distinction between sex romance and love. Students fall in and out of love. They have crazy emotions, have to make decisions to engage in sexual activity or not, and to stay in relationships, even long distance. And many are breaking up with their high school sweethearts—their first love. Protagonist Darius Lovehall dedicates his poem to Nina Moseley, who he meets at the poetry bar. When reciting "A Blues for Nina" aka "Brotha to the Night," Darius reveals two phrases: "Who Am I?" and "Cause rather than deal with the fallacy of this dry ass reality, I rather dance and romance your sweet ass, in a wet dream," implying he does not want to deal with reality. His reality: searching for an identity and trying to distinguish between sex, romance, and love is a reality many young adults face. In a *General Theory to Love*, Thomas Lewis claims, "Who we are and who we become depends, in part, on whom we love" (Lewis, 2000: 144). Hence the poems in the movie help define love and who Darius and Nina become based on whom they love. When Nina realizes, she loves Darius, at the close of the movie, she response to him as she recalls the possibility of love, reciting the poem, "I am remembering love" originally written by Sonia Sanchez (Sanchez, 1999: 10). *Love Jones* teaches the student how poetry can define, explain, and illustrate one word, in this case love. Definition is a rhetorical pattern in which the student writer learns to explain a word, object or idea so that the reader or listener knows as precisely as possible what the writer means (Flachmann & Flachmann, 2014: 356). *Love Jones* teaches first year students to subjectively define a term that is abstract, complex and controversial—love. Once again poetry points to truth as the student understands it as well as teaching them to define their topic with details.

Not every student understands poetry, wants to write poetry, or even believes poetry is important. Poetry for the reader or the writer speaks truth and dares to explore our humanity, something easily masked and suppressed. Many first-year writing students rarely learn to express their uncertainties or elations in their writing. As a result, they need a space to ask questions, and engage in deep reflection, and even find a gateway to other forms of writing. Students believe they understand writing because they have spent their early years writing essay after essay, learning the bones of writing but not learning how to give the work a heart and muscle; therefore, teaching them to look at poetry as a way to tell a story, and a way to insert one's self into an assignment, like a research paper, reflects a new perspective. I understand that not every English professor likes *Dead Poets Society* arguing Mr. Keating, the poetry teacher at Welton Academy, doesn't analyze poems in its entirety; but that's not the point of the movie. Not even in my classroom. The movie looks at the Welton students living in the footsteps of their parents, even parents living through their parents' identity. The movie defines poetry based on humanity and perspective not textbook theory and societal expectations.

When Mr. Keating stands upon the desk, he tells the students:

> I stand upon my desk to remind myself that we must constantly look at things a different way. The world looks very different up here. Just when you think you think you know something you have to look at it in another way. When you read, don't just consider what the author thinks, you must consider what you think.

At this moment, Keating teaches the students in his classroom that poetry is like life, when one thinks they understand something it's important to look at that something another way, change their perspective considered what they think. In my classroom, this scene teaches students that poetry is not simply rhyming words or abstract meaningless words and image, but poetry can tell a story.

On the second day of class, Mr. Keating tells the class the objective of the course when he says, "We don't read and write poetry because it's cute. We read and write poetry because we are members of the human race. The human race is filled with passion. Medicine, law, business, and engineering are noble pursuits and necessary to sustain life. But poetry, beauty, romance, love, these are what we stay alive for." Here, Mr. Keating sets the stage explaining that poetry is important because we are humans with feelings, emotions—fear, grief, joy, and victory.

One semester, G., a student, refused to write or even read the selected poetry. Adamantly, he said poetry should rhyme, if it's not Shakespeare it's not poetry. Then we read and listened to Willie Perdomo's rap poem "123rd Street Rap" (Perdomo, 1996: 15). Perdomo illustrates a street in Spanish Harlem with sounds and rhythm, sadness, and hope, with brevity and clarity. Alliteration—bullets bounce, stoop steps—added rhythm of rap and quickened the pace of the poem. G. changed his perspective exclaiming, "This is my block, this is my street. Poetry isn't just Shakespeare." As a result, the student understood that poetry could relate to one's identity, feelings, and environment. Like Mr. Keating standing on the desk to remind himself that things change, G. learned something new about poetry.

2   The Autobiographical Poem: Childhood Memory

The motif of identity continues with the autobiographical poem. I assign an autobiographical poem before assigning the autobiographical narrative essay. Poems teach students that all forms of writing benefit from the powerful and concise phrases found in poems (Simmons, 2014). The autobiography poem demonstrates how a poem can tell a story about one moment in the writer's life that comes from a childhood memory. The memory should connect to the student's topic because when it does part of the poem can become part of the essay. The memory also gives the student a different perspective about their topic. The poems used for this assignment are Rita Dove's "Fifth Grade Autobiography" (Dove, 1989: 8) and Anne Sexton's "Fury of Overshoes" (Sexton, 1973: 30). Both poems are childhood memories and independence. The first-year writing student sometimes struggles with independence and identity. Therefore, these two poems illustrate how to use symbols and images to explain struggles and hurdles as they are coming to age.

"Fifth Grade Autobiography" illustrates a nostalgic childhood about family. The speaker, a fifth grader, describes her family at a lake in Michigan. The speaker reflects on a photograph captured when she was four years old and recollects the personalities and memories of her grandparents and her brother. The poet uses language and imagery that describes time, place, and emotions. "Fifth Grade Autobiography" shows the student how to write about one specific moment, in a specific place with specific people and specific emotions. In this case jealously, "I am staring jealously at my brother" (line 17), perhaps, the loss of a loved one "I was strapped in a basket/behind my grandfather. /He smelled of lemons. He's died—/But I remember his hands" (lines 19-22). This poem shows the student to capture a memory with smell and touch as the speaker sees her grandfather using his left hand to touch the tobacco in pocket, sun printing luminous paws on grandmother's dress, and the smell of lemons. As a result, students explore and discover how their past shaped their identity, affects their present and influences their future.

"Fury of Overshoes" is a childhood memory of overshoes that symbolize growing up. The memories like "Fifth Grade Autobiography" are nostalgic. The young child wears overshoes that take her through life and its wonders. Various images in the poem point to the speaker of the poem working hard to achieve goals, such as:

> buckle your own
> overshoe
> or tie your own
> overshoe
> or tie your own shoe
> or cut your own meat
> and the tears
> running down like mud
> because you fell off your
> tricycle?
> (lines 5–15)

Each achievement is something new. The overshoe helps student focus on a symbol with several layers of meaning about growing up. Once again students can look at how their past shaped their identity.

3   Joe Brainard's I Remember Poem in the I-Search Paper

The I-Search paper is a personal research paper about a topic that is important to the writer. An I-Search paper is usually less formal than a traditional research paper; it tells the story of the writer's personal search for information, as well as what the writer learned about the topic. When writing the I-search paper, students have to have a personal connection to the topic, the specific issue. Students have written about grief that stemmed from loss of a parent, school suicide and grief counseling, cooking as a healthy craft, and what it means to be black in the age of black lives matter. I have discovered this assignment decreases plagiarism; a student should find it immoral and difficult to plagiarize another's lived experience. A section of the I-Search paper requires the student to write an *I Remember* poem, imitating Joe Brainard's infamous poem *I Remember*, used "wherever writing courses are taught, for children, college students, or very old and the results never fail to summon up long-forgotten particulars of lived experiences" (Brainard, 2010: xvii). In the introduction of *Collected Writings of Joe Brainard,* Paul Astor notes that Brainard's poem is a "composition method" that serves as an "organizing principle," which helps the "writing take off." The exercise involves writing the words I remember, and "as if a magic formula" students will "remember and remember with a clarity and specificity" how they became acquainted with their topic. For example, one student's topic was the glass elevator. His "I remember" poem recalled being a child standing on his grandmother's front porch in Chile gazing at the stars. The student's "I Remember" poem becomes part of her I-Search paper. The poem can be placed in the beginning, middle or at the end of the paper. This gives the student the freedom to decided where the poem is most effective in the I-Search paper.

4   Conclusion

Poetry is difficult to sell, especially to first-year writing students who think that they know everything about writing or know nothing at all. But as the student navigates through different mediums in the classroom such as film, stream of consciousness, and autobiography I create a more enticing environment to learn about poetry and how it can be used as a tool for self-discovery, and a space for self-expression. The student learns more about their topic of interest using poems with varied subject matters because they are challenged to use imagination and become active participants rather than passive learners. One Dutchess Community College student resisted imitating poetry, saying she was a poet and wanted to write her style. However, at the end of the poetry workshop unit she thanked me for the opportunity to learn different poetic structures and forms. And when it comes to the poetry changing the hearts of students who consider poems emotional crap a culinary student wrote the following: "So it was quite disappointing when Mrs. Hooks assigned this project to us. As I was forced to do this project, I learned that every time I wrote a poem that it hit a somewhat emotional nerve inside me. Even though I thought the project as a whole was a waste of time, I realized every time I had to write poetry I always made sure it meant something and came from a sentimental place in my heart. I have accumulated five poems that give a slight insight to my life and where I came from with my family's upbringings and mentality." This culinary student's newfound understanding of poetry mirrors Robert Penn Warren's quote: "For what is a poem but a hazardous attempt at self-understanding: it is the deepest part of autobiography." A student's self-understanding often points back to the method of letting the student choose their topic in which they have a personal connection. For example, one student wrote in the reflection section of her I-Search paper that choosing her own topic gave her the freedom to write about whatever she wanted, as long as she had support to back up her claims. She wrote, "I am really glad to have learned about myself." In regards to the autobiographical narrative, one student didn't enjoy the assignment. During the end of the class syllabus review, she said, "Writing about the autobiographical narrative taught me that I don't really know myself." When it comes to teaching the first-year writing student, my goal is to keep them engaged, writing, and learning by any means necessary whether we're imitating poetry, talking back to the poets or dissecting films to discover how poetry works as narrative.

References

Alderson, Daniel. (1996). *Talking back to poems: A working guide for the aspiring poet.* Berkeley, CA: Celestial Arts Publishing.

Brainard, Joe. (2010). *The collected writings of Joe Brainard.* New York, NY: Henry Holt.

Brown, Rita Mae. (2014). Writing as a moral act. In Kim Flachmann & Michael Flachmann (Eds.), *Prose reader: The essays for thinking, reading, and writing* (10th ed.). Boston, MA: Pearson.

Dierking, Rebecca. (2002). Creative copying, or defense of mimicry. *The Quarterly, 24*(4), 7–11. Retrieved January 30, 2018, from https://www.nwp.org/cs/public/print/resource/448

Dove, Rita. (1989). *Fifth grade autobiography in grace notes.* New York, NY: W.W. Norton & Company.

Flachmann, Kim, & Flachmann, Michael. (2014). *Prose reader: The essays for thinking, reading, and writing* (10th ed.). Boston, MA: Pearson.

Ginsberg, Allen. (1956). *Howl and other poems.* San Francisco, CA: City Light Books.

Hugo, Richard. (1979). *The triggering town, lectures and essays on poetry and writing.* New York, NY: W.W. Norton & Company.

Kincaid, Jamaica. (1978, June 26). Girl. *The New Yorker*, p. 29.

Lamott, Anne. (1994). *Bird by bird: Some instructions on writing and life.* New York, NY: Pantheon Books.

Lewis, Thomas. (2000). *General theory of love.* New York, NY: Random House.

Oliver, Mary. (1994). *A poetry handbook: A prose guide to understanding and writing poetry.* New York, NY: Harcourt.

Perdomo, Willie. (1996). 123rd street rap. In Willie Perdomo (Ed.), *Where a nickel cost a dime* (pp. 15–17). New York, NY: W.W. Norton & Company.

Sanchez, Sonia. (1999). *Shake loose my skin: New and selected poems.* Boston, MA: Beacon Press.

Sexton, Anne. (1973, January 27). The fury of overshoes. *The New Yorker*, p. 30.

Simmons, Andrews. (2014, April 8). Why teaching poetry is so important. *The Atlantic.* Retrieved from http://www.theatlantic.com/education/archive/2014/04/why-teaching-poetry-is-so-important/360346

Tannen, Deborah. (2017). Deborah tannen on writing. In X. J. Kennedy, Dorothy M. Kennedy, Jane E. Aaron, & Ellen Kuhl Repetto (Eds.), *The Bedford reader* (13th ed.). New York, NY & Boston, MA: Bedford/St. Martins.

Warren, Robert Penn. (1985, May 12). Poetry is a kind of unconscious autobiography. *The New York Times.* (1923-Current File)

CHAPTER 6

"Thirsty Women and Fuckboys"
Teaching Shakespeare with Memes

Kathleen Alves

"One cannot expect positive results from an educational ... program which fails to respect the particular view of the world held by the people," Paolo Freire argues. "Such a program constitutes cultural invasion, good intentions notwithstanding" (Freire, 1970: 84–85). "Cultural invasion," in Freire's view, is an act of violence that constitutes an imposition of the dominant group's worldview on the oppressed, inhibiting creativity of the latter by silencing their unique modes of expression. Language and writing instructors who teach in linguistically, socio-economically, and culturally diverse classrooms engage in a pedagogical high-wire act: how does one balance a respectful acknowledgement of students' non-traditional expressions while meeting higher education objectives of traditional knowledge modes without committing an act of cultural invasion? And how does one do that teaching Shakespeare, whose work represents the high culture of Western literary tradition, but (for many of my students) whose works also evoke fear and terror of the difficult task untangling his esoteric poetic language?

I have attempted to harness students' unfamiliarity with Jacobean and Elizabethan material as an opportunity to introduce them to the texts and history of the period in an exciting way, notwithstanding their groans and moans at the thought of reading and writing about the Bard's work. I've discovered that contextualizing Shakespeare and making transhistorical connections to present-day concerns of love and relationships documented as internet memes on visual social media sites like Instagram and Twitter have been successful with student engagement, relating Helena's "How happy some o'er other some can be!" speech with the contemporary notion of "thirsty," or off-putting desperation, as an example. In this chapter, I discuss some of the difficulties I have encountered in teaching Early Modern poetry in the introduction to literature survey course (student engagement, underpreparedness, second language learners) at Queensborough Community College of the City University of New York, and the inclusive pedagogical methods I have adapted to bridge previous student knowledge drawn from social media with traditional modes of learning valued in four-year schools.

1   The Problems: Student Underpreparedness and Relevance without Reduction

At most community colleges, including Queensborough, the majority of students can be categorized as non-traditional: mature, international, recent immigrant, and first-generation (American Association of Community Colleges). Students who attend community college comprise the largest undergraduate population in America. As institutions that offer accessibility, flexibility, and lower tuition fees, two-year schools appeal, and are dominated by, "nontraditional" students. Nontraditional students are those who do not fit the classic profile of young people living in dorms, their school fees paid by their parents. As the pressure to acquire a college degree has increased over the last few decades—as a prerequisite for the job market, for example—so has the number of nontraditional students who enter with handicaps: academically underprepared, impoverished, disability diagnoses, juggling jobs and family commitments. And while these students make up the largest demographic, they are the most at-risk for dropping out of school. In fact, a perverse pattern exists in postsecondary educational hierarchy: students whose lives and social disadvantages receive less guidance, structure, and resources than their counterparts at selective colleges. While there are many promising programs implemented at Queensborough Community College like the Accelerated Study in Associate Program (ASAP), learning communities, mentoring programs, and academic support services like the Campus Writing Center, these methods have not raised the graduation rate to the national average. The national three-year graduation rate for associate students at public 2-year institutions is 20%. In my home state, New York, it's 21.4%.[1] For cohorts who entered in the Fall of 2008, the City University of New York reported a 13.5% graduation rate, a difference of 61% from the national average.[2] These initiatives, while showing moderate success, support mainstream knowledge over non-traditional knowledge. Inclusive teaching may bridge this gap; inclusive teaching, pedagogy that incorporates both minority and mainstream cultures, encourages non-traditional students to engage with the material and learn traditional North American academic skills through the instructor's recognition of their unique knowledge modes. This approach is especially effective in teaching traditional works, or the canon, to non-traditional students. You can't get more "dead white guy" than Shakespeare.

Like Julian Hermida, I believe that students are not underprepared, that "their preparation reflects the world around them" (Hermida, 2010: 19). Students' preparedness and the way they see themselves reflect their own cultures, traditions, and beliefs. Chinese students, for example, are taught never to question or evaluate those in authority, like their professors, which clashes with the dialogic ethos of the North American classroom (Arkoudis, 2006). The North American teaching model is neither better nor worse than other instructional paradigms, but it is generally presented as the only way of generating, organizing and expressing thought in our colleges (Bowden & Marton, 2004: 250). This model can be characterized as external, socially mitigated, and objectively measurable (Haigh, 2009: 273). Composition instruction is reduced to teaching thesis-based writing (Bean, 2011: 116). Critical thinking displaces other forms of thinking, such as creative and integrative (Boyer, 1997: 95). North American knowledge modes have been criticized as elitist, exclusive, and patriarchal in its distortion of other ways of acquiring knowledge (Bean, 2011: 56).

Teaching literature from a wider array of diverse traditions can yield the richest degree of learning and student success. Students are more enthusiastic to learn mainstream North American ways of thinking and expressing if they are presented as one of many alternatives of interpretation, creation, and expression (Bowden & Marton, 2004: 191). The major goal for teachers in two-year schools is to prepare students for transfer to four-year colleges where traditional knowledge modes are predominant. Inclusive teaching, then, allows students to be interested enough to adopt these skills.

Concentrating on the learning styles and needs of the two-year college student and the cultural diversity of the community, my inclusive pedagogy is informed by Freire's process of promoting conscientization and aims to bridge learner's life experiences with instruction for meaning and relevance. Contextualizing Shakespearean texts and bridging transhistorical connections to contemporary and familiar media forms like memes have produced positive outcomes with student engagement, which can be the most challenging obstacle in teaching two-year college English courses. Cognitive studies have shown that to learn a new idea, students must link the idea back to the familiar. The more that new material can be connected to the familiar foundation of personal experience, the easier it is to understand (Zull, 2002: 82). Thus, I frequently turn to pop culture references to foster knowledge processing and acquisition with unfamiliar material.

Some younger students imagine texts produced before the age of Drake the rapper as part of some esoteric past peopled with speakers who spoke and thought in unfamiliar and inscrutable ways. Derek Longhurst echoes the concern for instructors of the Bard in *The Shakespeare Myth*, "How do we make it relevant?" (Longhurst, 1988) My students' inexperience and concomitant terror of reading Shakespeare is most apparent when we move from reading and writing about nineteenth and twentieth-century short fiction to Elizabethan verse and drama. For many of my students, this is the only course in which they will be immersed in literary study. Therefore, I am armed with this urgency to present literature and its context as accessible and relevant in order for students to meet general education and course objectives. In other words, if they do not understand what they are reading, or worse, if they don't *want* to understand, they will not be equipped to write about the course material.

Why insist on assigning a text in which students feel such aversion and, at times, downright hostility? First, the richness of the material in its complexity and apparent obliquity demands close reading and analysis, the foundation of critical thinking. The mysteries of the text require cutting open the body, examining its complex systems and its simple cells under a slide, to discover revelations of the human condition. Marjorie Gruber notes, "Shakespeare has scripted many of the ideas that we think of as 'naturally' our own and even as 'naturally' true: ideas about human character, about individuality and selfhood, about government, about men and women, youth and age, about the qualities that make a strong leader" (Garber, 2008: xiii). The challenge in teaching Shakespeare—the complexity of characters, themes, dramatic structures, and poetic techniques—is also its strongest benefit to student learning. Literature that has made the most profound impact on its readers is complex because, to put it simply, our lived reality is complex. Instructors seek to help students acquire the skills necessary to succeed not only in the classroom, but also beyond the brick buildings of the college campus. Learning to understand and unpack complexity is essential to navigating the confusing and overwhelming terrains of our complicated lives. Reducing Shakespeare in order to breeze through the material, to fulfill our educational obligations of having taught his work in higher education, is a severe pedagogic limitation of developing and sharping students' skills to think critically and analyze literary works and human psychology. My students often express shock upon learning that Shakespeare's plays, such as *Hamlet* and *Henry V*, are commonly used as training tools for corporate executives! (Ibid., xix).

Second, studying Shakespeare provides students the opportunity to tackle difficult material with more confidence and perseverance. Short fiction's comprehensible plot and grammatical structure is easy enough to follow and can be, in fact, "skimmable." However, poetry insists on the reader's absolute attention and meticulous care. One word, in a line of seven, can suddenly be pregnant with a multiplicity of meanings. This is not to say that this is absent in prose, only that impatient readers are most likely to miss it. The slow process of disentangling unusual sentence structures, recognizing and comprehending poetic compressions, omissions, and wordplay, reading the notes to archaic word definitions and unfamiliar allusions produces a deeper understanding of the works' complexities and an enduring memory of the play itself, as well as of the process of learning.

But why use Internet memes? Incorporating memes in pedagogy is my way of avoiding the "cultural invasion" Freire warns us against. For many of my students, and perhaps, for many Americans in general, Shakespeare represents a pleasure enjoyed by the intellectual elite. The antagonism between highbrow culture (i.e. Shakespeare and the opera) and lowbrow culture (i.e. pulp films and comic strips) have created clearly defined camps equally disdainful of the other; the beau monde sneers at the uncultured philistine, and in turn, the populists roll their eyes at the pretentiousness of the high and mighty snobs nestled in cushy ivory towers. Through the democratic nature of the Internet, I aim to reconcile these camps and show that Shakespeare can be—and does—occupy both modes of populist pulp that gouges out eyes and makes crass dick jokes, and of deep philosophical and metaphysical reflection. High and low art converge through the study and creative engagement of his work.

For Patrick Davison, "an Internet meme is a piece of culture, typically a joke, which gains influence through online transmission" (Davison, 2012: 122). Limor Shifman describes them as "cultural information that passes along from person to person, yet gradually scales into a shared social phenomenon" (Shifman, 2013: 364). Memes harness the "key logics," as Shifman calls it, of Internet culture: sociability, replicability, and participation. According to Claudia Leigh, memes spread via a social bond and circulate through ubiquitous communication mediums like Gchat or Facebook (Leigh, 2009: 131–141). In other words, an Internet meme is a funny image or video that is replicated and spread quickly by Internet users.

Internet memes can be dismissed as a lowbrow art form, yet they have massive influence on culture. And, in many ways, these memes give a political voice to the people through the creative act. Though some Internet memes are passively circulated viral pictures or gifs, others encourage user engagement through iteration, imitation, parody, and satire that can reproduce numerous variants. Memes are the raw material for creativity; the website memegenerator.net allows users to caption, then share, popular images. The study of memes recalls the study of television or popular music a generation ago, but with a difference: media scholars argue that memes exemplify the shift from a consumption culture to one of production. Teenagers of the MTV and BET generation would sit in front of their boxy TVs, watching "Total Request Live" or "106 and Park." In contrast, today's youth would engage directly with popular culture, contributing to the conversation by overlaying a witty caption over a photo of the Dos Equis "The Most Interesting Man in the World," or "Success Kid," or "Leonard di Caprio's Cheering Great Gatsby." Media scholar Clay Shirk observes that the simplest, most shallow humor emerging from memes is still a product of creative work (Shirky, 2010). Writing on the subject of memes, Alice Marwick argues, "Memes are the closest thing to a native cultural form the Internet has, and, as such, they demonstrate the sprawling variety of the medium" (Marwick, 2013: 12–13).

Internet memes are easily generated by "meme generators" online, so any Internet user can create one for public circulation. Margaret Wertheim observes that cyberspace can be imagined as a utopian space beyond history—paradoxically not existing in a physical state yet existing in the tangible social space for its users. Particularly, the ideal feature of the Internet is its erasure of bodily markers, open to everyone regardless of age, sex, gender, nationality or class (Wertheim, 1999: 283). Furthermore, Mark Poster extols cyberspace's democratization in that it encourages multidirectional discourse without the constraints of face-to-face communication (Poster, 1997: 201–202). Anonymity and accessibility encourages creators to be more daring, to create caustic and sharp satire, for there is no tangible fear of accountability.

Richard Dawkins coined the term "meme" in his 1976 book, *The Selfish Gene*, to detail how cultural information is disseminated throughout society primarily through imitation (Dawkins, 1989: 192). He compared the rapid evolution of fashion and customs with the ways genes evolve. Investigating how influential norms could turn on a dime, Dawkins categorized cultural products into units called memes, including "tunes, ideas, catch-phrases, clothes fashions, ways of making pots or of building arches" (Ibid., 192). In similar fashion as gene propagation from body to body, Dawkins notes, "memes propagate themselves in the meme pool by leaping from brain to brain via a process which, in the broad sense, can be called imitation" (Ibid.). If I hear a great joke, I pass it on to my friends, family, colleagues and students, then they pass it on to more people. If the joke catches on, it can be said to replicate itself from brain to brain. For Dawkins, memes, like genetic variants, must possess three key elements for successful propagation: copy-fidelity, fecundity, and longevity. Copy-fidelity is the meme's ability to replicate; fecundity is the speed of its replication; and longevity is its stability over a period of time. Certain memes will have more success than others if they fit a cultural need or are distinctively appropriate to a specific circumstance, what Dawkins calls a "survival value" (Ibid., 193). Internet memes have high copy-fidelity and fecundity qualities, but extremely low longevity. They pop in and pop out of culture, becoming irrelevant and obsolete days later. Part of the pleasure of Internet meme culture is being in on the joke, on time.

A meme's copy-fidelity echoes the literary principles in Aristotelian Poetics, in which humans are considered to be mimetic beings, that our urge to create texts or art to reflect and represent our reality is innate, and that the act of imitation in itself is pleasurable (Aristotle, 2013: 347). In this way, creating art (through Internet memes for example) is a means of attempting to comprehend our own realities. In 2013, Dawkins described Internet memes as a "hijacking of the original idea," repurposing a notion in subversive ways (Dawkins, 2013). Memes are intertextual by definition, accumulating and generating meanings across texts, all meanings depending on other meanings created in alternative contexts. They are a manifestation of the Habermasian ideal, in which claims of truth are subjected to rational arbitration rather than determined by the power of vested interests (Habermas, 1989: 222–235). Therefore, juxtaposing highbrow, canonical works with "uncultured" forms not only showcases the depths of Shakespeare's influence on postmodernity, it is also a political choice that defends the voice of the populace, in the sense of the Bakhtinian *carnivalesque*. As Donald Hendrick and Bryan Reynolds have noted in *Shakespeare without Class: Misappropriations of Cultural Capital*, Shakespearean drama is a "socially and historically determined playground" and "an ambiguous space that makes possible and in fact encourages alternative opportunities for thought, expression, and development" (Hendrick & Reynolds, 2000: 11). Truly, instructors must set Shakespeare free from the shackles of the intellectual elite, and find a means of opening a space in which he speaks to everyone, and everyone can speak to him.

2   The Solution: Harnessing Previous Knowledge to Bridge Connections

Before transitioning to *Hamlet*, the final and longest text my students will read for the semester, I cull four or five well-known speeches from Shakespeare's works, including *The Tempest*, *Othello*, and *Macbeth*, to "practice" how to read Shakespearean language. After the first year teaching *Hamlet* cold, I have discovered the necessity in preparing students with strategies for reading and understanding Elizabethan writing styles; I have a handout with "tips," including reading inverted phrases and sentences, considering punctuation and contracted language, and looking up obsolete, archaic, or unfamiliar definitions. After reviewing the handout, we apply these tips to the short speeches. For the purposes of this chapter, I will focus on Helena's Lament in *A Midsummer Night's Dream* to explain how I incorporate social media in helping student comprehension of the material in the text as well as its greater thematic concerns of love, blindness, and deception.

First, I give the students a comically reduced plot summary of the play, focusing on Helena and Demetrius' love melodrama: Hermia loves Lysander, but her pops Egeus wants her to marry Demetrius. Helena is Demetrius' ex and still loves him, though he jilted her for Hermia. Egeus gets the law involved and basically Hermia has to marry Demetrius or live her life as a nun for the goddess Artemis. Hermia and Lysander escape into the forest, and Helena narcs on them to Demetrius, hoping he'll change his mind about Hermia. Fairies like Oberon the Fairy King and his jester Puck get involved, love potions are administered, and the rest is comedy.

We read the speech aloud twice: once for familiarity, twice for meaning.

> How happy some o'er other some can be!
> Through Athens I am thought as fair as she.
> But what of that? Demetrius thinks not so;
> He will not know what all but he do know:
> And as he errs, doting on Hermia's eyes,
> So I, admiring of his qualities:
> Things base and vile, folding no quantity,
> Love can transpose to form and dignity:
> Love looks not with the eyes, but with the mind;
> And therefore is wing'd Cupid painted blind:
> Nor hath Love's mind of any judgement taste;
> Wings and no eyes figure unheedy haste:
> And therefore is Love said to be a child,
> Because in choice he is so oft beguiled.
> As waggish boys in game themselves forswear,
> So the boy Love is perjured every where:
> For ere Demetrius look'd on Hermia's eyne,
> He hail'd down oaths that he was only mine;
> And when this hail some heat from Hermia felt,
> So he dissolved, and showers of oaths did melt.
> (Shakespeare, 1993: ls. 232–251)

I ask students to jot down what they believe to be the general idea Helena expresses; no close reading yet, just their first visceral reaction. Most can pick up on Helena's tone of self-pity and anger that Demetrius loves Hermia though all of Athens considers her "as fair as [Helena]." For most students in the class, she cuts a pathetic figure, desperate for love that is not reciprocated. One student has asked, "Doesn't she have any self-respect?" Even students who feel a pinch of sympathy for her case suggest that "she should move on." After a brief discussion on their initial impressions, I invite students to work in groups to engage in closer reading by exploring the speech's use of metaphors. First, what is Helena saying about love? Second, how is desire expressed through these metaphors?

The theme of "sight and blindness" is present in *Midsummer Night's Dream* and Helena refers to this idea five times in her speech. The first and second is where Demetrius is "doting on Hermia's eyes," and where he "looked on Hermia's eyne." This is important since Hermia's eyes captivate Demetrius, but later his eyes are blurred by Oberon's love nectar. The third reference, "Love looks not with the eyes but with the mind," is ironic for Oberon instructs Puck to place the nectar on Demetrius's eyes so that he falls in love with the first thing he sees. In this case, love does see with the eyes, not with the mind. "Winged cupid painted blind," the fourth reference, infers that love is blind. The last reference, "Wings, and no eyes, figure unheedy haste," insinuates that loving a person without seeing who they are really are is as dangerous as flying blindly. The contradiction of the meanings between "unheedy" and "haste" illustrates this impossible circumstance.

At first, students are quick to point out that Shakespeare uses the "Love is blind" cliché to express Helena's frustrated desire. This notion is accessible enough, but I push the students to think further about humans as sexual subjects, specifically Helena's characterization and positioning in the power dynamics of love in the play.

At this point, I present students with a series of memes of the "thirsty" woman on the projector. This move usually elicits laughter; I assume the humor lies in the cultural shift from the high art of Shakespeare to the lowbrow meme. Or perhaps it is the Professor's lame attempt to be "with it"? Whatever the reason, it refreshes the energy in the classroom and invigorates student engagement.

I pull up the familiar "Maury Lie Detector" meme. Maury Povich and his tabloid talk show, *Maury*, have become synonymous with trashy theatre. Affecting a laughably transparent demeanor of compassion, Povich exploits the relationship issues of mostly poor women of color. Paternity testing and lie detector tests are two of the most popular topics of the show, with each case concluding with Maury reading the "results" off a show card. The meme is a shot from the show that captures this dramatic "moment of truth" recognizable to viewers. For the class, I pull up this meme with this caption in familiar block lettering: "You said you're not thirsty for attention/Your Instagram determined that is a lie."

The next meme is the "Correction Guy." In this black and white image, an elegantly suited man makes a "stop" gesture with his hand. This meme is often accompanied with a caption correcting some kind of faux pas or social error. Here, the captions read, "Stop being thirsty/It's not cute."

The term "thirsty" has been in popular circulation for a few years now and its colloquial meaning builds on the familiar definition of showing a strong desire for something, i.e. "thirsty for power." The positive connotation of passionate ambition is reversed in the slang sense. Someone who is "thirsty" is almost always in the context of human contact and communication, a person who is desperate or seeking attention in a pitiful way. There is no preposition in this case; one is just "thirsty." It is a desire that can never be quenched, for the desire itself is off-putting.

The fascinating feature of this kind of "thirst" as a classification of human desire is that it dooms itself. The display or expression of genuine interest or love is almost immediately dismissed for its intense authenticity. The popular disdain for "thirstiness" advocates a restrained and moderate articulation of desire.

Back to Helena. I ask my students to reconsider the representations of amatory passion through the language of the meme: Is Helena "thirsty"? If so, does this help explain Demetrius' rejection of her love? What does Shakespeare seem to be saying about the power dynamics of love and desire here? Her first line, "How happy some o'er other some can be," can be read as an outburst of self-pity. The second line, "Through Athens I am thought as fair as she," expresses her jealousy and pride. Upon a closer examination of the theme of seeing and blindness through the metaphors, students discover that Helena's desperation—by accusing Demetrius of being blind—ironically illustrates her own blindness, her refusal to see that her own wretchedness and yearning for love is off-putting. Students point out that the Maury meme's point of uncovering a hidden truth—in this case, a person's self denial—speaks strongly to the tragically conspicuous and myopic desperation of a rejected lover. The fantastic bit to witness here is how students, through careful consideration of language and poetic devices, critically evaluate a character's contradictions and complexities. Through a robust and energetic discussion and debate about the paradox of love's "unheedy haste" in the speech and in their lives, they unpack layers upon layers of meaning to arrive at a synthesis of a character's psychology and of a culture's orientation in the power dynamics of love and desire. One female student had blurted out, "This is why it's so hard to be real with people!"

This exchange is an example of students illustrating their "deep reading." According to Judith Roberts and Keith Roberts, students need to be "deep readers" who focus on meaning (semantic memory), rather than "surface readers" who focus on facts and data (episodic memory). Deep reading requires a psychological engagement with the text: "A good reader forms visual images to represent the content being read, connects to emotions, recalls settings and events that are similar to those in the reading, predicts what will happen next, asks questions, and thinks about the language. One of the most important steps, however, is to connect the manuscript [they] are reading with what [they] already know and to attach the facts, ideas, concepts, or perspectives to the known material" (Roberts & Roberts, 2008: 126). "Deep reading" bridges the familiar with the unfamiliar, enabling students to comprehend and retain difficult material. I have run into past students in the hallway who ask me if I still use memes in my class, which shows me that the exercise is memorable.

Next, we move from Helena to Demetrius. Who is this guy? What did he do for Helena to "catch feelings" so intensely? "Catching feelings" is another neologism, which means the process of unavoidably falling in love in which the person loses self-possession. "Catching feelings" is considered to be a negative event, for the loss of control also entails the lowering of emotional defenses, increasing the risk for heartbreak. For this, we look at the flashback section in the speech in the final four lines. Helena compares Demetrius' display of love for her to hail. Hail, cold and harsh, is usually not associated with the heated passion of love, such as the sun or fire. This signals that Demetrius' love was not genuine, for his "showers of oaths did melt" when "some heat from Hermia's [he] felt" (l. 251, 250). I present a new series of memes and ask my students, "Is Demetrius a Fuckboy?"

Unlike "thirsty," "fuckboy" has an array of meanings and has been around for at least a decade. Explaining how dating apps like Tinder have changed the power structure of hookup culture, Nancy Jo Sales writes, "A 'f-ckboy' is a young man who sleeps with women without any intention of having a relationship with them or perhaps even walking them to the door post-sex. He's a womanizer, an especially callous one, as well as kind of a loser" (Sales, 2015). At its most general, the word is a catch-all term for a contemptible male.[3] A "fuckboy" is repellent to women for his insensitive duplicity, feigning love for the promise of sex.

I present the first image, the "One Does Not Simply …" meme. The meme has a close-up still of Boromir from the film, *Lord of the Rings: The Fellowship of the Ring* (2001), when he points out to the Fellowship of the difficulty of their proposed plan to destroy the ring: "One does not simply/walk into Mordor." Users fill in whatever suits their message and the moment in the second half of the caption. One user wrote, "One does not simply/watch one episode" to speak to the new binge-watching culture of Netflix; another user captioned, "One does not simply/buy one thing at Target" to address the inexplicable phenomenon of the full cart at the store's checkout line. In the meme I exhibit, the caption has been revised to state, "One does not simply/fuck with a fuckboy." When I ask students what this caption means to them, they chuckle and roll their eyes before telling me that the picture says two things: On one level, one does not simply, or *should not*, mess with this kind of guy. On another level, one does not *simply* engage with a fuckboy, that the entire enterprise will be exhausting and complicated. One should stay far, far away from this kind of man, but if you do allow him into your life, be prepared for the drama and baggage he will bring.

The second image I show is the "Titanic Rose" meme. In the image, a still shot from the 1997 film *Titanic*, an elderly Rose begins the story of her experience on the ship by saying, "It's been 84 years ..." The meme is generally used to indicate the slow passage of time, whether in a state of anticipation, or waiting for or dreading of something happening. For example, "It's been 84 years/waiting for the next season of Game of Thrones" or "It's been 84 years/since the semester started." For the class, the caption on this meme reads, "It's been 84 years/Me trying to find a man who isn't a Fuckboy." Most of my female students nod in confirmation to the meme's general message that most of the men that women encounter in their dating lives are deceitful rakes.

So, is Demetrius a "fuckboy"? To answer this question, I ask the class to read the last four lines closely: "For ere Demetrius look'd on Hermia's eyne,/ He hail'd down oaths that he was only mine;/And when this hail some heat from Hermia felt,/So he dissolved, and showers of oaths did melt." Helena concludes her speech with a melancholy retrospective of her past with Demetrius. Shakespeare's wordplay of "hail" illustrates Demetrius' unjust treatment of Helena and its consequences to her psyche. Before Hermia, Demetrius "hail'd down oaths," or acclaimed enthusiastically, of his exclusive love for Helena. Then, figuratively drawn as pellets of frozen rain, these declarations of love were melted by Hermia's "heat," thus dissolving these vows and, consequently, their relationship. Overall, hail is an apt metaphor for Helena's pain, caused by Demetrius' duplicitous display of love for Helena; hail unexpectedly arrives in a loud fury from the skies and leaves destruction in its wake. At this point, the class' general opinion of Helena shifts from contempt to empathy. She has become victim to Demetrius' deception because she could not see him for what he truly is—a misleading philanderer—still, she cannot help herself from desiring him: "How happy some o'er other some can be!" This complex dilemma of her "catching feelings" is highly relatable to many of my students; some share their experiences with heartbreak or fear of commitment because of the fuckboy trap.

In this moment, which is highly rewarding for me to witness, students who previously believed that Shakespearean language and works were completely inaccessible now have built a deep connection. With the help of social media and bringing in their own experiences into the reading, students unlock the puzzle of Shakespeare and, what's more, understand his value in modern culture. My hope, in every class, is to repel "cultural invasion" by inviting students to read the texts—as difficult as they may be at first—through their own worldviews and in their own language. Relating their own experiences through the reading is crucial; it is a demonstration of the reciprocal value between reader and text. The reader values the text for the truths it reveals about his or her reality, and in turn, the text values the reader for giving voice to the truths in that reality. As Roland Barthes has stated in his seminal essay, "The Death of the Author:"

> The reader is the space on which all the quotations that make up a writing are inscribed without any of them being lost; a text's unity lies not in its origin but in its destination. Yet this destination cannot any longer be personal: the reader is without history, biography, psychology; he is simply that *someone* who holds together in a single field all the traces by which the written text is constituted .... Classic criticism has never paid any attention to the reader; for it, the writer is the only person in literature ... we know that to give writing its future, it is necessary to overthrow the myth: the birth of the reader must be at the cost of the death of the Author. (Barthes, 1977: 148)

While I am not quite yet ready to kill off Shakespeare, Barthes' major point that the reader decodes and vivifies the written text absolutely informs my pedagogy at Queensborough. For many of my students who come into my classroom feeling defeated and disempowered in their own academic capabilities for a myriad of reasons (i.e. poverty, trauma, negligence), giving them back their power through their own terms and through their own experiences is crucial to bridging the gap.

3 Conclusion

Essentially, this is a low-stakes exercise of close reading and analysis that encourages students to move beyond a superficial response to the text. This practice is repeated and reinforced throughout the semester. After this class on focused reading, students are more equipped to read and write about *Hamlet*, students taking on more sustained reading and engaging with more complex themes that attempt to explain the complexities and contradictions of the human condition. Students do not merely "translate" Shakespeare—reducing its work into fragments—they engage in how language attempts to articulate the perplexities of what it means to be human, how we view ourselves, our realities, and the art we create to help us work through that understanding. As Michael Whitmore, Director of the Folger Shakespeare Library attests, "If we look only to markets, algorithms, and biology to show us the mysteries of the human heart, we will only get so far. We still need these powerful, adaptable, indispensable stories to teach us who we are" (LoMonico, 2016: 146).

Notes

1 United States. Dept. of Education—National Center for Education Statistics, "Retention of first-time degree-seeking undergraduates at degree-granting post-secondary institutions, by attendance status, level and control of institution, and percentage of applications accepted: 2006 to 2012," accessed January 19, 2015. https://nces.ed.gov/programs/digest/d15/tables/dt15_326.30.asp
2 City University of New York—Office of Institutional Research and Assessment, "Institution Retention and Graduation Rates of Full-time First-time Freshmen in Associate Programs by Year of Entry:* Queensborough," accessed January 19, 2015. http://www.cuny.edu/irdatabook/rpts2_AY_current/RTGI_0001_FT_FTFR_ASSOC_COMM-QB.pdf
3 The term also has circulation in gay male culture with a variety of meanings: i.e. submission in sex or a wealthy man's "kept boy" (Brogan, 2015).

References

American Association of Community Colleges. *Students at community colleges.* Retrieved January 19, 2015, from https://www.aawccnatl.org

Aristotle. (2013). *Poetics.* (Anthony Kenny, Trans.). Oxford: Oxford University Press.

Arkoudis, S. (2006). *Teaching international students: Strategies to enhance learning* (Unpublished manuscript). Centre for the Study of Higher Education, University of Melbourne, Melbourne. Retrieved from http://www.cshe.unimelb.edu.au/resources_teach/teaching_in_practice/docs/international.pdf

Barthes, Roland. (1977). *The death of the author* (Stephen Heath, Trans.). London: Fontana Press.

Bowden, John & Marton, Ference. (2004). *University of learning: Beyond quality and competence.* New York, NY: Routledge.

Boyer, Ernest. (1997). *Scholarship reconsidered: Priorities of the professoriate.* San Francisco, CA: Jossey-Bass.

Brogan, Jacob. (2015, August 18). "What is the Ff—kboy?" *Slate.* Retrieved March 6, 2017, from http://www.slate.com/blogs/lexicon_valley/2015/08/18/what_does_fuckboy_mean.html

City University of New York. Office of Institutional Research and Assessment. *Institution retention and graduation rates of full-time first-time freshmen in associate programs by year of entry: Queensborough.* Retrieved January 19, 2015, from http://cuny.edu/about/administration/offices/ira/ir/data-book/current/retention-graduation/system.html

Davison, Patrick. (2012). The language of internet memes. In Michael Mandiberg (Ed.), *The social media reader* (pp. 120–134). New York, NY: New York University Press.

Dawkins, Richard. (1989). *The selfish gene.* New York, NY: Oxford University Press.

Dawkins, Richard. (2013, June 22). Just for hits. *The Saatchi & Saatchi new directors' showcase* (video). Retrieved from http://www.YouTube.com/watch?v=GFnixX9edg

Freire, Paolo. (1970). *Pedagogy of the oppressed.* New York, NY: Bloomsbury.

Garber, Marjorie. (2008). *Shakespeare and modern culture.* New York, NY: Anchor.

Habermas, Jurgen. (1989). *The structural transformation of the public sphere.* Cambridge: MIT Press.

Haigh, Martin. (2009). Fostering cross-cultural empathy with non-western curricular structures. *Journal of Studies in International Education, 13*(2), 271–284.

Hendrick, Donald, & Reynolds, Bryan. (2000). *Shakespeare without class: Misappropriations of cultural capital.* New York, NY: Palgrave.

Hermida, Juan. (2010). Inclusive teaching: An approach for encouraging non-traditional student success. *The International Journal of Research and Review, 5,* 19–30.

John Bean. (2011). *Engaging ideas: The professor's guide to integrating writing, critical thinking, and active learning in the classroom.* San Francisco, CA: Jossey-Bass.

Leigh, Claudia. (2009). Lurkers and lolcats: An easy way from out to in. *Journal of Digital Research & Publishing, 2,* 131–141.

LoMonico, Michael. (2016, July). Teaching Shakespeare 400 years later. *CEA Critic, 78*(2), 146–147.

Longhurst, Derek. (1988). You base football player: Shakespeare in contemporary popular culture. In Graham Holderness (Ed.), *The Shakespeare myth* (pp. 59–73). New York, NY: Manchester University Press.

Marwick, Alice. (2013). Memes. *Contexts, 12,* 12–13.

Poster, Mark. (1997). Cyberdemocracy: The internet and the public sphere. In D. Porter (Ed.), *Internet culture* (pp. 212–228). London: Routledge.

Roberts, J. C. & Roberts, K. A. (2008). Deep reading, cost/benefit, and the construction of meaning: Enhancing reading comprehension and deep learning in sociology courses. *Teaching Sociology, 36,* 125–140.

Sales, Nancy Jo. (2015, August 6). Tinder and the dawn of the 'dating apocalypse'. *Vanity Fair.* Retrieved March 6, 2017, from https://www.vanityfair.com/culture/2015/08/tinder-hook-up-culture-end-of-dating

Shakespeare, William. (1993). *A midsummer night's dream*. New York, NY: Washington Square Press.

Shifman, Limor. (2013). Memes in a digital world: Reconciling with a conceptual troublemaker. *Journal of Computer-Mediated Communication, 18*(3), 362–377.

Shirky, Clay. (2010). *Creative surplus: Creativity and generosity in a connected age.* New York, NY: Penguin.

United States Department of Education. National Center for Education Statistics. *Retention of first-time degree-seeking undergraduates at degree-granting postsecondary institutions, by attendance status, level and control of institution, and percentage of applications accepted: 2006 to 2012.* Accessed January 19, 2015.

Wertheim, Margaret. (1999). *The pearly gates of cyberspace: A history of space from dante to the internet.* Sydney: Doubleday.

Zull, J. E. (2002). *The art of changing the brain: Enriching the practice of teaching by exploring the biology of learning.* Sterling, VA: Stylus.

CHAPTER 7

In Deference to Dreams Deferred
Langston Hughes' Poem, "Harlem (A Dream Deferred)" and Its Application across the Curriculum

Alice Rosenblitt-Lacey

"What happens to a dream deferred?" asks Langston Hughes in the first line of his famous poem, "Harlem." His poem can be used an interpretive lens to illuminate the themes of some of our most famous and popular plays, especially plays about science, technology, engineering and mathematics (STEM). This creates a valuable opportunity to teach poetry across the curriculum as Hughes posits a series of similes as possible answers to his initial question:

> What happens to a dream deferred?
>
> > Does it dry up
> > like a raisin in the sun?
> > Or fester like a sore—
> > And then run?
> > Does it stink like rotten meat?
> > Or crust and sugar over—
> > like a syrupy sweet?
> >
> > Maybe it just sags
> > like a heavy load.
>
> *Or does it explode?*

(All quotes from "Harlem" in this chapter are from the poem as it appears on the Poetry Foundation website: https://www.poetryfoundation.org/poems/46548/harlem.) This chapter examines the teaching of Langston Hughes' poem, "Harlem" (also known as "A Dream Deferred") in an English Department/Liberal Arts Seminar at LaGuardia Community College/CUNY on the topic of "Humanism, Science and Technology." In this interdisciplinary course, students examine how themes of Hughes's poem inspired the title and concepts of Lorraine Hansberry's (1930–1965) famous play, *A Raisin in the Sun* (1959) and how his poem's themes connect to the theme of social justice which is central to several other plays as well, particularly STEM-themed plays such as *Galileo* (1938) by Bertolt Brecht (1898–1956); *Arcadia* (1993) by Tom Stoppard (b. 1937); and *Proof* (2001) by David Auburn (b. 1969). The students in my course consider what might happen to the dreams of individuals living in a society which lacks equality of race, class and/ or gender due to prejudice and other forms of social injustice. Does a dream of achieving social justice "dry up/Like a raisin in the sun?" (Hughes, lines 2–3). This encourages students to consider the themes of Hughes's poetry to make connections between literature and the sciences and to show the relevance of poetry across the curriculum as Hughes's message of taking action to achieve a dream by challenging the status quo can be seen as applicable to many disciplines.

An important connection can be made between the "dream deferred" of Hughes's poem "Harlem" and that of a "dream job" or desired career path that often remains on hold while a college student completes a degree that prepares him or her to pursue that career after graduation. Many of our students share the "American Dream" of obtaining a well-paying job in their chosen career. I have at times tried to involve their dreams in a discussion of Hughes's poem which connects to the topic of poetry across the curriculum. In an urban college setting like New York City's public university system, there is much diversity in the student body in terms of race, religion, age, and other demographics. For example, there are many "non-traditional" older students. LaGuardia Community College/CUNY is located in Queens, one of the most culturally diverse counties in the entire country. One factor that can be seen as unifying this diversity is the students' desire to graduate from college.

Hughes's poem can be used to forge a bond amongst students across the curriculum who share this pursuit of the American Dream as they pursue their college degrees, despite the numerous differences in their majors or fields of study. A class discussion of their "deferred" dreams can help engender a sense of community in the classroom and beyond, as students share the obstacles they encounter in the pursuit of their dreams/dream jobs. I have asked students to complete a brief in-class writing exercise (lasting about 15 minutes) describing these obstacles. Some of their obstacles were the obvious: the years of schooling still ahead; the financial demands of a college education and of graduate school afterward; meeting their living expenses; time management challenges while balancing work, school and family obligations; the need for more experience, skills or certification in the field; the lack of connection to a professional network in the field; and competition with others in the field. Yet other obstacles they mentioned were more of a psychological nature and included self-criticism, self-doubt, lack of self-confidence, and the fear of self-disappointment. Some of these might be connected to the pressures of parental expectations and/or the lack of their parents' emotional support that many students experience. As students recognize what they have in common with their classmates, they can develop a certain respect for one another and their similar struggles which creates an atmosphere in the classroom more conducive to learning. Students also struggle with feelings of isolation and alienation which this in-class activity counters as students share their written responses with one another, helping them to feel less alone, more motivated, and more supported by their classmates.

As part of this in-class writing exercise, students were asked to identify similes from Hughes's poem that they might use to describe their feelings about their deferred dreams. Others, for "extra credit," opted to write their own similes which expressed mixed feelings about the future ranging from anticipation to trepidation. Some students focused on the more positive aspects of the promise of the future and the hope for new opportunities that it brings; its transformative possibilities; the desire for the ultimate feeling of satisfaction from the achievement of their goals; and the potential for helping others in the process. Others emphasized the negative aspects of the future including feelings of frustration, uncertainty or even trepidation about what the future might bring, perhaps due to fears of failure; vacillation about their career choices and wondering if these are indeed the "right" choices or even realistically attainable goals; frustration and impatience with the time it takes to work toward these goals; uncertainty about their own level of commitment to their choices; uncertainty about knowing themselves well enough to know what they really want; fear of success and if it would be too much to handle; and the time needed to get more maturity and certainty regarding their choices.

My students' majors range from the health professions (nursing, medicine, OT, PT, etc.) to computer science and to science and engineering; from the fine arts to education and to law and law enforcement; and from business to accounting and to the social sciences and social work. Only a few of my students are planning to major in English, yet we are studying various works of literature together in this course. When we discuss their "dreams deferred," it brings students across the curriculum together as they connect their lives and experiences to poetry via Hughes's question, "What happens to a dream deferred?" This unity in diversity is a most advantageous outcome of teaching poetry across the curriculum and one that Hughes would applaud in its recognition of our shared humanity. Indeed, he would applaud this striving for unity through verse at the university!

Other teachers have documented their own use of Hughes's poetry for similar purposes. Timothy Patrick Moran in his article, "Versifying Your Reading List" published in *Teaching Sociology*, describes a course he teaches on the topic of "inequality": "To help my students see that race and racial oppression encompasses everyone, I use two of Langston Hughes' more famous poems, 'I, Too' and 'Harlem'" (Moran, 1999: 118). He recommends teaching Hughes's poem "Harlem" across the curriculum as he does in his sociology class, as he notes that "'Harlem' is a good poem for undergraduates to read because it plays off the popular notion of 'the American Dream'" (Ibid.: 119). The critic Allison Kerns concurs as she discusses what she terms "the (so-called) American Dream" of "many Americans who believed that through hard work and determination, they could achieve prosperity" (Kerns, 2007: 47). Kerns further points out that "Hughes recognized not only this promise of a dream but also its relative inaccessibility to his peers, primarily because of race .... In 1951, Hughes published the poem, 'Harlem' (also known as 'A Dream Deferred') in *Montage of a Dream Deferred* and made famous his comment that postponed and unrealized dreams lead to pain and devastation" (Ibid.: 47). Moran further describes how he teaches this poem "as a class, we go through each of the similes, interpreting them as representing a variety of reactions people have to inequality (in order—cynicism, anger, denial, hopelessness and resistance)" (Moran, 1999: 119) further analyzing the categories of "pain and devastation" to which Kerns alludes. Critics agree that "the poem 'Harlem' is a response to dreams of freedom from an American who did not see this as a country where dreams could come true, but rather as where people of African descent were denied freedom ..." (*Harlem*, 1998: 64).

Moran pairs the reactions to a "dream deferred" with the similes of Hughes's poem as follows:

"Does it dry up/like a raisin in the sun?"—cynicism
"Or fester like a sore—/And then run?"—anger (as escape?)
"Does it stink like rotten meat?"—anger (as self-destruction?)
"Or crust and sugar over—/like a syrupy sweet?"—denial
"Maybe it just sags/like a heavy load."—hopelessness
"Or does it explode?"—resistance

Based on my conversations with my students about this poem, a few more reactions can be further added to pair with these similes:

"Does it dry up/like a raisin in the sun?"—resignation
"Or fester like a sore—/And then run?"—persistence; multiplication
"Does it stink like rotten meat?" —demand for attention
"Or crust and sugar over—/like a syrupy sweet?"—success; anticipation
"Maybe it just sags/like a heavy load."—depression; exhaustion
"Or does it explode?"—usurpation; removal; destruction

Jemie, the Nigerian critic, gives a different reading of some of these images. He sees the similes as alternatives to anger: "rather than turning to anger, frustration could dry up, fester, stink, crust and sugar over" (Ibid., 65). Harry Phillips agrees that instead, these are "questions that aim to immerse the reader in the imagery of despair and disappointment" (Ibid., 69). Specifically, instead of reading, "Does it stink like rotten meat?" (line 6) as an image of anger, Jemie sees this line as a reference to a "lynched black man rotting on the tree" (Ibid., 67–68). He also sees the following simile, "Or crust and sugar over—/like a syrupy sweet?" not as denial as Moran suggested but rather as a symbol of "all of the broken promises of Emancipation and Reconstruction, of the Great Migration [and] integration ..." (Ibid., 68). Lenz agrees with Jemie that Hughes wrote about "economic and social and political discrimination ... of the present problems of the 'Harlem of the bitter dream'" (Lenz, 1988: 331). Phillips asserts that "nearly all critics of 'Harlem' interpret the 'dream' in the poem's opening section as a symbol of African Americans' desire for equality—social, economic, and educational—in American society. That this desire is 'deferred' means that African Americans continue to endure the difficulty realities of racism and limited opportunity in a presumably free society" (*Harlem*, 1998: 69).

My students tend to see some of these similes in a more optimistic light than these critics do, as my students see the beauty of the symmetrical crystalline structure of the "syrupy sweet" as a symbol of the potential for the hope of achieving satisfaction and success in life. They also have interpreted "fester like a sore" as somewhat positive in its persistence which could lead to success as it multiplies, spreads, and revives.

The discussion of Hughes's poem leads us directly to a study of Hansberry's famous play which draws its title from one of Hughes's similes. Many of my students feel a close identification with Beneatha Younger from *A Raisin in the Sun* as she is also a college student dedicated to the pursuit of her goal to become a doctor. The Youngers, an African-American family living in the poverty and segregation of post WWII Chicago's South Side, have had their dreams of a better life "deferred" due to the obstacles of racism, classism and sexism. Beneatha's struggles help us to address these obstacles in the course. Beneatha, as a young African-American female college student, dreams of going to medical school in spite of her brother, Walter, and his sexist mocking of her dreams as he urges her to become a nurse instead of a doctor or to just get married instead of pursuing any career. Beneatha also confronts financial obstacles which threaten to defer her dream when Walter loses the money their mother had told him to put aside for Beneatha to attend medical school. Beneatha's dream seems to "dry up/like a raisin in the sun" until her conversation with Joseph Asagai from Nigeria, a fellow college student, helps to restore some of her resolve to continue to pursue her dream of becoming a doctor and to be one of "... those who see the changes—who dream, who will not give up" (Hansberry, 1988: 134).

In addition, Beneatha's mother's dream of moving out of the ghetto with her family almost did "dry up/Like a raisin in the sun" after she buys a house in Clybourne Park, an all-white neighborhood, only to be told by Karl Lindner, representing those living there already, that "Negro families are happier when they live in their own communities" (Ibid., 118) and that they should not move into neighborhoods where they "just aren't wanted" (Ibid., 119). However, Hughes's poem concludes with another alternative for "What happens to a dream deferred?" (line 1), i.e. *"Does it explode?"* (line 11). The "explosion" posited by Hughes could take the form of an individual challenging the status quo by means of social protest or action. "Eventually ... the road to civil rights did lead to an explosion of violence, just as 'Harlem' foretold" (*Harlem*, 1998: 65). Onwuchekwa Jemie, the famous Nigerian critic and author of *Langston Hughes: An Introduction to the Poetry*, "interprets the poem as a militant outcry against racial injustice. Jemie argues that the images in the poem build in intensity until 'the violent crescendo at the end'" (Ibid., 67). It is true that in "Harlem," Hughes certainly

> guides us, through his use of images and similes, to a deeper acknowledgment of African Americans' disillusionment with the American dreams of seizing opportunity, working hard and enjoying success ... The poem's final line contrasts mightily with the tone of earlier questions. It is designed both to shock and enlighten readers as to the explosive spirit and drive fueling an American dream and a determined people ... It also underscores, emphatically, that the repressed, but still throbbing, dream of equal treatment will indeed be realized ... we note in this eleven-line poem the poet's ability to skillfully blend history and art with the politics of resistance. (Ibid., 69–71)

One example of such a group of people determined to realize their dream of equal treatment is the Younger family as they, in the end, reject the request (and the financial offer) made by Lindner as the representative of the "Welcoming Committee" of Clybourne Park. The undeterred Youngers will move to this all-white neighborhood because, as Walter declares, "My father—he earned it for us brick by brick" (Hansberry, 1988: 148). Beneatha may decide to pursue her dream of becoming a doctor in Africa. Here, "dreams deferred" can ultimately lead to action, and that action can in turn lead to restoring social justice as an individual challenges the status quo.

This theme of an individual challenging the status quo raised by the final question in Hughes' poem can be extended across the curriculum as students in this course are encouraged to make connections between individuals challenging the status quo in *A Raisin in the Sun* and in other plays such as Bertolt Brecht's play, *Galileo;* Tom Stoppard's play, *Arcadia;* and David Auburn's play, *Proof,* where mathematicians and scientists also challenge the status quo, be it racism, sexism or other societal beliefs. Bertolt Brecht's play, *Galileo,* is a work we read in our "Humanism, Science and Technology" seminar that suggests another possible way of dealing with "a dream deferred." This play is set in 17th-century Italy, as Galileo espouses the heliocentric theory of the universe, previously proposed by Copernicus, in which the sun is believed to be the center of the universe. Galileo is met by grave opposition from the Catholic Church which still promoted the geocentric concept of the universe favored by Aristotle in which the earth was believed to be the center of the universe. With the aid of the newly invented telescope, Galileo proves the geocentric model to be scientifically invalid, polarizing science and religion.

Conveniently, almost every scene in Brecht's play is introduced by a short poem, making a conversation about how poetry can be connected to science even more apropos. For example, Scene 1 begins: "In the year sixteen hundred and nine/Science's light began to shine/... Galileo Galilei set out to prove/The sun is still, the earth is on the move" (Brecht, 1966: 47). This allows *Galileo* to be a wonderful vehicle for teaching poetry across the curriculum. I often break my class into small groups and each group is assigned a scene or two from this play. The students are asked to consider the connection of the poem that introduces their scene(s) to the action that occurs in that part of the play. After the groups meet, they summarize their answers on the board in one or two sentences and also write a quote from the dialogue in their scene(s) for support. Then we regroup by organizing their desks into a circle and each group presents its answers to the rest of the class.

Through this close reading of Brecht's play, we see how Galileo is forced to recant his theories after being threatened with torture by the Inquisition and put under house arrest for the last decade of his life until his death in 1642. Although he is allowed to pursue his scientific writings at home, he is forbidden to disseminate his work. At the end of Brecht's play, Galileo's former research assistant, Andrea, comes to visit him. Galileo reveals to Andrea that even though "my superiors ... lock my pages away as I dictate them ... I wrote the 'Discorsi' out again during the night" (Ibid., 120). He gives Andrea the completed manuscript of the *Discorsi* which, in the final scene of the play, Andrea smuggles out of Italy to be published abroad. Here then is an example of an individual challenging the status quo in a more subversive manner.

Publicly, he pretends to follow the authority of his day and their demands but privately, he refuses to allow his dream of publishing his scientific writings to be "deferred" preventing it from "drying up like a raisin in the sun" and instead secretly counters the Church's instructions. Students can be asked in class to discuss if they think that any of the other similes that Hughes lists in his poem can be used to describe Galileo's sub-rosa subversion of the status quo. They can also be asked to evaluate the effectiveness of this approach of "quietly" challenging the status quo. For instance, maybe his dream was one that did "crust and sugar over—/Like a syrupy sweet?" (lines 6–7) as Hughes suggests, with the false sweetness of feigned acquiescence.

The sociologist Timothy Moran interprets this line of Hughes's poem as indicative of a form of "denial" (Moran, 1999: 119), however, though Galileo may have seemed to be denying his dream, perhaps this was only a public pretense while he still secretly held onto his private determination to pursue this dream. Students can explore how individuals may challenge the status quo by proposing new ideas either by way of poetry and literature, as Hughes does, or by way of new scientific theories and discoveries, and how this results in a society which may progress by both avenues. Inspired by a critique of social injustice and oppression which may cause "dreams deferred," as expressed in Hughes's poem, students are encouraged to consider how we can extend the impulse to challenge our social perspectives through poetry to mathematical or scientific inquiry and beyond.

One play that looks at a challenge of contemporary sexism is the Pulitzer prize-winning play by David Auburn, *Proof*. Its fictional female protagonist, Catherine, is a mathematical genius who has made a ground-breaking discovery by writing a proof about prime numbers. Other mathematicians at first doubt that she is the true author of this proof, partially due to the sexist assumption that a *woman* just could not have had this brilliant an insight and that in general they are just not as talented or gifted as men in the field of mathematics. Like Beneatha Younger in Hansberry's play, Catherine is a young woman determined not to let sexism defer her dream of pursuing her chosen career. Beneatha's own brother, Walter had counseled her to give up her dream of becoming a doctor and urged her instead to "go be a nurse like other women—or just get married and be quiet ..." (Hansberry, 1988: 38). However, Beneatha in *A Raisin in the Sun* differs from Catherine in *Proof* because of the additional obstacles that Beneatha faces in the forms of racism and classism. Beneatha, as an African-American working-class woman, confronts the intersection of prejudice based on her race, class and gender, unlike Catherine, a white middle-class woman, who is not as bound by the obstacles of race and class. Unfortunately, however, both Beneatha and Catherine do encounter sexism as women in traditionally male dominated fields.

In Auburn's play *Proof* we see Catherine dealing with sexism as a woman in STEM during a conversation with Hal, a mathematician who is Catherine's love interest in the play. Hal tells Catherine that in their field, the "original work—it's all young guys" and when Catherine calls him on this, repeating "Young guys" he corrects himself and says, "Young people." Catherine acknowledges, "But it is men, mostly" (Auburn, 2001: 35). Hal tries to align himself more with Catherine by saying

Hal:	There are some women.
Catherine:	Who?
Hal:	There's a woman at Stanford. I can't remember her name.
Catherine:	Sophie Germain.
Hal:	Yeah? I've probably seen her at meetings, I just don't think I've met her.
Catherine:	She was born in Paris in 1776.
Hal:	So I've definitely never met her …. I'm stupid. Sophie Germain, of course.
Catherine:	You know her?
Hal:	Germain Primes.
Catherine:	Right.
Hal:	They're famous. Double them and add one, and you get another prime. Like two. Two is prime, double plus one is five: also prime.
Catherine:	Right. Or $92{,}305 \times 2^{16.998} + 1$.
Hal (*startled*):	Right.
Catherine:	That's the biggest one. The biggest one known …. (Ibid., 35–36)

Here, Catherine demonstrates her impressive mathematical knowledge with a spontaneous display of her familiarity with Germain primes. While it is true that there are fewer women in STEM than men, and it is not sexist to say so, Hal's inability to recall the name of the "woman at Stanford" is dismissive of this woman and her accomplishment of being affiliated with this prestigious university. Hal's example of a Germain Prime also assumes that Catherine has at best a rudimentary understanding of mathematics as he uses the simplest illustration, the number 2. Catherine's counter-example, the largest known Germain prime, "startled" Hal in its complexity, as Auburn's stage directions indicate. Her spontaneous use of this example is proof that she obviously has this unusual bit of information committed to memory! Catherine is clearly both well informed and passionate about mathematics, despite the challenges of being a woman in this male-dominated field.

Catherine's description of Sophie Germain's experience as a female mathematician situates Catherine's own experience within the historical context of sexism toward women in math and science and within the patriarchy in general:

> Catherine: She was trapped in her house. The French Revolution was going on, the Terror. She had to stay inside for safety and she passed the time reading in her father's study. The Greeks .... Later she tried to get a real education but the schools didn't allow women. So she wrote letters. She wrote to Gauss. She used a man's name. Uh—Antoine-August Le Blanc. She sent him some proofs involving a certain kind of prime number, important work. He was delighted to correspond with such a brilliant young man .... (Ibid., 35)

Like Galileo, Catherine's dream of making a significant contribution to the field of mathematics was undeterred by obstacles she faced. Though both faced different obstacles in different branches of STEM, they both pursued their own research and made original discoveries at night "in secret."

Catherine dropped out of college to live at home and take care of her mentally-ill father. The only time she had to work on her mathematics was at night, after he went to bed, as she tells Hal at the end of the play, recounting to him her experience of writing the proof:

> Catherine: ... It was just connecting the dots. Some nights I could connect three or four. Some nights they'd be really far apart, I'd have no idea how to get to the next one, if there was a next one.
> Hal: He really never knew? [referring to Catherine's father]
> Catherine: No, I worked after midnight. He was usually in bed. (Ibid., 82)

Galileo, too, successfully copied over the pages of the *Discorsi* in secret at night. Galileo, Catherine and the Youngers, though characters of different time periods, all refused, either overtly or covertly, to allow their dreams to be permanently abandoned, even if those dreams were temporarily deferred by their societal obstacles. Perhaps if a "dream deferred" does "explode," it is the best possible outcome, as it may result in social change? Gunter Lenz agrees that the final lines of Hughes's poem "Harlem" describes what he terms "resistance" and was "thus anticipating the 'riots' of the 1960s" (Lenz, 1988: 331). The Civil Rights movement could be seen as the collective "explosion" of a "dream deferred," the dream of racial equality that could not ever begin to become a reality until segregation finally "exploded" in America.

As in Moran's course, in my course on "Humanism, Science and Technology," we also study social inequality and the individuals who challenge such inequality by challenging the status quo. We make connections between the social inequality of racism and the social inequality of sexism by looking at several other plays, notably the one-act play "Trifles" (1916) by Susan Glaspell (1876–1948); *Top Girls* (1982) by Caryl Churchill (b. 1938); and *Arcadia* by Tom Stoppard. I usually begin the semester by having students read "Trifles" aloud on the first day of class. Glaspell's one-act is easily available online at *Project Gutenberg.org* and can be read aloud in class within an hour. "Trifles" is an excellent vehicle for introducing the topic of sexism in the early 20th-century. In this play, Minnie Wright is suspected of murdering her husband, ironically named Mr. Wright. The local Sheriff, his wife, and the County Attorney have arrived at the Wrights' farmhouse, the scene of the crime, to investigate and try to find a motive. The Wrights' neighbors, Mr. and Mrs. Hale, are also present. The topic of sexism quickly arises as the Sheriff dismisses the need to examine the downstairs of the Wrights' farmhouse. After the County Attorney asks him, "You're convinced that there was nothing important here—nothing that would point to any motive?" the Sheriff answers, "Nothing here but kitchen things." The Sheriff is also surprised to hear that Minnie Wright had been concerned about her jars of fruit exploding in the cold weather, an explosion prefiguring the exploding of a dream deferred that Hughes would suggest half a century later. The Sheriff exclaims, "Held for murder and worryin' about her preserves" and Mr. Hale explains, "Well women are used to worrying over trifles" (Glaspell, *Trifles*). The sexist assumption of the men that the "kitchen things" are unimportant is subverted in Glaspell's play as Mrs. Hale and Mrs. Peters, the wives of the neighbor and the sheriff, respectively, discover case-breaking clues downstairs, in and near the kitchen, as the men investigate elsewhere.

The men mock the women's observations, including the fact that Mrs. Wright was sewing a quilt. When the men come from upstairs and overhear Mrs. Hale saying, "I wonder if she was goin' to quilt or just knot it?" the Sheriff repeats Mrs. Hale's question and the stage directions describe how then "*The men laugh, the women look abashed.*" The stage directions also indicate that Mrs. Hale states "*resentfully*" to Mrs. Peters, "I don't know as there's anything so strange, our takin' up our time with little things while we're waiting for them to get the evidence" (Ibid.). Mrs. Hale has to some degree internalized the men's sexism, believing that as a woman she is concerned with the "little things" of life, with "trifles." Yet she and Mrs. Peters find clues in the downstairs areas of the house which provide a motive suggesting Mrs. Wright did indeed murder her husband. Thus, the title of Glaspell's play, "Trifles," is highly ironic, as the "little things," the "kitchen things" are actually the important clues which the men overlook completely, allowing the women instead to solve the case.

Glaspell's play "Trifles" provides a great segue into our class's next play, *Top Girls* by Caryl Churchill, which takes a look at feminism in the early 1980's. *Top Girls*, first published in 1982, also addresses sexism as Marlene, a successful woman in the corporate world, has just received a promotion to become the new managing director of her office. One of her male co-workers, Howard Kidd, is completely distraught that he has not received this promotion. Howard's wife visits the office to ask Marlene if she would decline the promotion so that Howard could have it instead. Mrs. Kidd informs Marlene that Howard did not come in to work that day because he was "in a state of shock. About what's happened" and Mrs. Kidd wonders, "What's it going to do to him working for a woman? I think if it was a man he'd get over it as something normal." Marlene, unaffected, replies, "I think he's going to have to get over it" (Churchill, 1984: 58). When Mrs. Kidd sees her attempts to persuade Marlene to relinquish the promotion are futile, she becomes enraged at Marlene, calling Marlene a "ball breaker," predicting that Marlene will "end up miserable and lonely," and declaring "You're not natural" (Ibid., 59). Just as in *Trifles*, we see some women in *Top Girls* have internalized the sexist assumptions of the patriarchy even while other women are challenging those sexist beliefs. Hughes's poem reminds us that, whatever the -ism is, when individuals challenge the status quo, they usually face societal backlash and may need to "explode" the oppressive norms to overcome social injustice (but we *shall* overcome, *some* day). The work is ongoing as the dream of equality for women, people of color, and people of the working class is still "deferred."

Beneatha in *A Raisin in the Sun* and Catherine in *Proof* who confront obstacles to their pursuit of careers in medicine, science or mathematics lead us in the course to read Tom Stoppard's play *Arcadia* where Thomasina Coverly confronts her own obstacles as an early 19th-century mathematical genius, a fictional character based on Ada Lovelace, the real-life daughter of the Romantic poet Lord Byron akin to the 20th-century genius Catherine of *Proof*. In *Arcadia,* Thomasina's discoveries are lost for almost two centuries. She is ahead of her time, as only toward the end of the 20th-century with its advent of computers is the true import of her discovery recognized. Thomasina (like the real-life Ada Lovelace, the 19th-century female mathematician often regarded as the first computer programmer) invents the basis for fractal geometry and its technique of iteration upon which modern day computing depends. In *Arcadia*, the invention of new computer technology leads society to new understandings of the universe, just as the invention of the telescope does in *Galileo*. Without a computer, Thomasina Coverly's paper-and-pencil graphs, hypotheses and calculations could only go so far, but Valentine, a graduate student in the sciences, in the play's 20th-century world, enters her formulas into his laptop and discovers the true brilliance of the "Coverly set" and her anticipation of the contemporary field of fractal geometry (an echo of the famous "Mandelbrot Set" discovered by Bernoit Mandelbrot, founder of the field of fractal geometry).

Not only does *Arcadia* contain a character based on the Romantic poet Lord Byron's daughter but also a fictionalized portrayal of Byron himself is present during the 19th-century scenes of the play. Though he never appears on stage, his many exploits are narrated while he is a guest at the Coverly estate, most notably, his affair with Mrs. Chater, one of the other house guests. In one of the 20th-century scenes of the play, Valentine enters into a debate with a literature professor named Bernard about the merits of science vs. the merits of poetry. Bernard quotes from Lord Byron's famous poem, "She Walks in Beauty," in order to prove his argument that literature is equally as relevant as science to our lives, if not more so! In Scene 5 of *Arcadia*, Bernard becomes offended when Valentine "casually" says that "it's all trivial anyway ... who wrote what when ..." and Bernard vehemently objects: "Trivial? ... I'm sorry—did you say trivial?" (Stoppard, 1993: 64) Bernard continues in defense of literature and the humanities: "A great poet is always timely. A great philosopher is an urgent need ... If knowledge isn't self-knowledge it isn't doing much, mate" (Ibid., 65). Then Bernard quotes the first four lines of Byron's poem, "She Walks in Beauty," to prove his point: "'She walks in beauty, like the night of cloudless climes and starry skies; and all that's best of dark and bright meet in her aspect and her eyes'" (Ibid., 65–66). The beauty of this poetic verse indeed clinches the debate in Bernard's favor and on behalf of the arts in general.

Though the debate here is between science and poetry, even the characters themselves acknowledge that neither they nor these disciplines are really so diametrically opposed. In that regard, Bernard and Valentine are ultimately in concurrence with the idea of poetry across the curriculum, as Valentine himself admits that Bernard is "not against penicillin, and he knows I'm not against poetry" (Ibid., 66). Even Byron's imagery of the "beauty" of the "starry skies" could be seen as symbolic of a union of poetry and science. Byron's references to "bright and dark" can be interpreted as the pursuit of knowledge that lights our journey through the unknown, be it through scientific inquiry or through literature and self-discovery. In fact, creativity is the unifying variable applying poetry across the curriculum, connecting literature and scientific/mathematical inquiry. It is the path we all must tread to progress, to grow and to pursue new discoveries, be they personal, scientific, social or political.

Langston Hughes reminds us that "dreams deferred" can still have the potential to be "explosive" and instrumental in challenging the status quo. Thus, the "darkness" of social inequality—racism, sexism and the like—can be factors spurring the "brightness" of valuable social growth—in a union of what Byron describes as "all that's best of dark and bright ... thus mellowed to that tender light." That "tender light" is often described in poetry as the light of scientific knowledge, as it was by Brecht as he concludes *Galileo* with a wonderful poetic couplet that in and of itself applies poetry across the curriculum: "May you now guard science' light,/Kindle it and use it right ..." (Brecht, 1966: 129). The "right use" of science and mathematics can be examined by using poetry across the curriculum as Hughes's poetry encourages us to consider social justice and when and where it is lacking, to think creatively to challenge such injustices of the status quo.

References

Auburn, David. (2001). *Proof*. New York, NY: Faber and Faber.
Brecht, Bertolt. (1966). *Galileo*. New York, NY: Grove Press.
Churchill, Caryl. (1984). *Top girls*. London: Methuen Drama.
Glaspell, Susan. (1876–1948). *Trifles*. Project Gutenberg.org [Web]. Retrieved February 21, 2017, from http://www.gutenberg.org/files/10623/10623-h/10623-h.htm.
Hansberry, Lorraine. (1988). *A raisin in the sun*. New York, NY: New American Library.
Harlem. (1998). Poetry for students In Marie Rose Napierkowski & Mary Ruby (Eds.), *Poetry for students virtual reference library* (Vol. 1, pp. 61–73). Retrieved February 21, 2017, from http://www.*PoetryforStudents*group.com/ps/i.do?p= GVRL.Literature&sw=w&u=cuny_laguardia&v=2.1&id=*PoetryforStudents*%7 CCX2690900014&it=r&asid=100d1416abadcb5ba690d8c92b59a389
Hughes, Langston. (1951). *Harlem (a dream deferred)*. PoetryFoundation.org. Retrieved February 21, 2017, from https://www.poetryfoundation.org/poems-and-poets/poems/detail/46548
Kerns, Allison. (2007). It was like a dream of hell: Gantian dreams deferred. *Thomas Wolfe Review, 31*(1–2), 47–61.

Lenz, Günter H. (1988). Symbolic space, communal rituals, and the surreality of the urban ghetto: Harlem in Black literature from the 1920s to the 1960s. *Callaloo, 35,* 309–345.

Moran, Timothy Patrick. (1999). Versifying your reading list: Using poetry to teach inequality. *Teaching Sociology, 27*(2), 110–125.

Stoppard, Tom. (1993). *Arcadia.* New York, NY: Faber and Faber.

PART 4

History

CHAPTER 8

Expressive Content Writing
The Inclusion of Poetry in Undergraduate History Courses

Frank Jacob

>   Rain, midnight rain, nothing but the wild rain
>   On this bleak hut, and solitude, and me
>   Remembering again that I shall die
>   And neither hear the rain nor give it thanks
>   For washing me cleaner than I have been
>   Since I was born into this solitude.
>   Blessed are the dead that the rain rains upon:
>   But here I pray that none whom once I loved
>   Is dying to-night or lying still awake
>   Solitary, listening to the rain,
>   Either in pain or thus in sympathy
>   Helpless among the living and the dead,
>   Like a cold water among broken reeds,
>   Myriads of broken reeds all still and stiff,
>   Like me who have no love which this wild rain
>   Has not dissolved except the love of death,
>   If love it be towards what is perfect and
>   Cannot, the tempest tells me, disappoint.

∴

1 Introduction

The above quoted poem, *Rain* by Anglo-Welsh poet Edward Thomas (1878–1917), is just one of numerous examples of World War I poetry. Since the beginning of the centennial for this "seminal catastrophe" (Kennan, 1979: 3) of the 20th century, historical studies related to the topic have increased[1] and teachers and educators around the world have sought to integrate an event that has long passed into their class sessions (Norris, 2005). In particular, history courses in senior high school and early college classes have helped to improve students' sensitivity for the First

World War, not only as a historical topic but also as a human experience. However, it seems sometimes difficult for the instructor to connect the students to events that happened so long ago, and contemporaries of the events can no longer be brought to the classroom to keep the events alive.[2] Consequently, I, as a history professor at a community college, was looking for a method (the use of poetry in the classroom, to be more precise) that could not only awaken the students' interest but would also combine different disciplines and, consequently, strengthen the abilities of the students beyond analyzing texts in the historical field.

In the following chapter I would like to share (1) the theoretical models considered while composing the course plan and (2) the practical experiences with the students, who were not only exposed to World War I poetry but also required to write their own works of poetry based on pior readings. In a third part, I will describe how these experiences were used during a pilot study, which will analyze the impact of the use of poetry and students' performances in an "Introduction to Modern East Asian Civilizations" course at Queensborough Community College during the Fall and Spring Semester (2016/17). While one class actively and/or passively (writing and/or reading) dealt with poetry as a text form for the whole semester, the control group in the second semester went through the course materials using other text forms. Based on the findings of this pilot study, which was financially supported by one of Queensborough Community College's CETL Challenge Grants, and which used poetry in different courses in the humanities (History, Philosophy, and Sociology), I hope to make the case for interdisciplinary approaches in the history classroom that combine the study of poetry as a text form and as the documentation of historical events. I hope to grant the students a better historical insight and develop in them empathy for topics that are hard to relate, to as the events themselves seem to lie too far in the past.[3]

2   Theoretical Approach

German pedagogues since the mid-1990s have criticized that texts are very often understudied in classroom environments since production-oriented practices (Haas, Menzel & Spinner, 1994: 17), that actually create something new instead of just re-interpreting already existent texts, are seldom used. Most text work is based on analyzing and interpreting existent texts to answer preconditioned questions that the teacher wants to get answered by the students. In history classes, in particular, the focus very often lies on sources, of which many have been published in extensive or condensed reader formats as well.[4] With regard to dominant text-related pedagogical methods, it was remarked that those who study should also be "addressed with regard to their sensitivity, their emotions, their phantasy, and their zest for action" (Haas, Menzel & Spinner, 1994: 17), something that could be achieved by the integration of poems into history classes where poems might help to establish an emotional contact to the matter of study.[5]

While emotion usually emerges "most clearly through reflective writing" (Rai, 2012: 270) and since, as Lucy Rai further remarks, "Reflective practice is becoming a common feature of many practice-based courses" (Ibid.), it is also important and possible to use an emotional reaction to stimulate the students' curiosity to more intensely focus on a topic in the classroom. Simply put, the emotion is no longer just used as the reflective instrument but also as the stimulating trigger that draws the students' attention toward the topic per se.

Existing poems will consequently be used as a first contact medium, and, by the transformation of these first hand texts,[6] the students are able to evolve their own impressions of the evidence by designing a new poem that is still connected to the overall topic of the First World War. Therefore, the history classroom becomes a creative writing class, yet the writing is content based, which means while the format is lyrics, the topics discussed in this specific form of writing remains attached to the overall topic of the course section dealing with the First World War. The students consequently are supposed to perform what I would like to call "expressive content writing." Of course, in order to do this, the professor will have to analyze the original poem in detail with the class. Due to this first step one also has to make clear that the students' texts are not devaluated by a comparison with the original (Haas, Menzel & Spinner, 1994: 23).[7] It has to be emphasized to the students that the attempt to rewrite should not create a reinterpretation of existing poetry but rather a student version of her or his interpretation of a war poem that might be connected to the events of the First World War. The students are then eventually drawn into the subject, as they have to critically and emotionally think about the situation of the soldiers that spent most of their time in the trenches, waiting for the next battle to take place. One of these combatants described the effects of modern weaponry on the soldiers and their bodies, which he found after an artillery assault: "I found them lying just a few yards away. They'd had their legs blown off and all I could see when I got to them was their thigh bones. I will always remember their white thigh bones. The rest of their legs were gone" (cited in Rennell, 2014). Combined with images of the trenches and the no-man's-land of World War I, the students get a better impression of the soldiers' situation on the Western Front between 1914 and 1918.[8] Nevertheless, the emotional level of the student seems to be better reached by reading poetry with them. This is why I experimented with this kind of approach in my Modern Western Civilization survey course at Queensborough Community

College in the past years. My initial assumptions have also been supported by the results of a study, which focused on teaching psychology in production-oriented manner (Raisch, 1998: 30–31).

In our case of First World War poetry it is not only the analysis of the poem that will have a decisive impact on learning outcome for the student but also the process to write one by her/himself. There is also another point that is extremely important. The classroom is an environment in which different people are studying together and therefore provides a natural or genuine diversity, especially in the New York metropolitan area, as it is so characteristic for the community colleges of the City University of New York.[9] By implementing production-oriented practices of learning, those students who need to develop emotional intelligence before they can develop an analyzing one (Raisch, 1998: 31) are better integrated into a classroom where their specific needs are not totally neglected by the simple focus on analyzing and interpreting texts following a preset formula. The emotional engagement will motivate students to take the risk to engage in something they considered boring or not worthy of their time before and probably also stimulate a further interest in the topics and materials discussed in the future. The possibility to "emotionally bind" the student to a topic consequently offers an attractive strategy to cause an interaction between pedagogy and learning in the environment of a history classroom.

In addition to the already named advantages of the integration of poetry into history classes the described method will help to improve several competences of the students, including their historical, aesthetic, and language competences (Ibid., 33–36). They usually will also develop a higher sensitivity for the processing of texts, encouraged not only by the analysis of the historical poem, but also by the task to write one on their own. At best, the analyzing of a World War I poem will not only strengthen the interest of the students in historical events but it will also help to improve their language skills and, thereby, their interest in poetry or other forms of literature that are connected to the studied events. All these aspects were identified during several attempts to include World War I poetry into history courses at Queensborough Community College. However, the approach is not limited to the community college level; it could be helpful for future curriculum development in K-12 or college courses in the history major in general, particularly in class sessions that deal with the First World War.[10]

3 Prior Experiences

In the classroom, the use of poetry, considering experiences in numerous courses, was a success. However, in my experience this success is a scafoding process. First of all, one course session will be needed to explain the First World War and its historical impact to the students in order to make them familiar with the historical dimension, especially with regard to the human losses that were created by the war in Europe and around the world. In a second step one could use documentaries or images of archaeological findings related to the events (Mullally, 2013: 40–42) to visualize the trench warfare in Europe to provide the students with an image of the war scenario from a soldier's perspective. Consequently, the poem itself will be just the final part of a program that might cover two to three classroom sessions.

Furthermore, the professor has to select World War I poems that are not too difficult to analyze and also offer a diverse perspective on the possibilities to describe a horrible event like the war on a massive scale. It turned out that the most effective poems in the courses were the above quoted "Rain" by Edward Thomas and "I Have a Rendezvous with Dead" by American poet Alan Seeger (1888–1916). While the first one gives a vivid impression of the life in a war environment like a trench by expressing the monotony of war itself, it also provides a good example to explain the use of metaphors—like rain in this particular case—as a rhetorical tool. The analysis of Seeger's poem adds a second step, as the image of the spring in the poem can be interpreted in several ways: the endlessness of the war, the inevitability of death, or the start of a battle when the soldiers are leaving their trenches beneath the ground like flowers that start to flourish in the spring.

I Have a Rendezvous with Death

> I have a rendezvous with Death
> At some disputed barricade,
> When Spring comes back with rustling shade
> And apple-blossoms fill the air—
> I have a rendezvous with Death
> When Spring brings back blue days and fair.
>
> It may be he shall take my hand
> And lead me into his dark land
> And close my eyes and quench my breath—
> It may be I shall pass him still.
> I have a rendezvous with Death
> On some scarred slope of battered hill,
> When Spring comes round again this year
> And the first meadow-flowers appear.

> God knows 'twere better to be deep
> Pillowed in silk and scented down,
> Where love throbs out in blissful sleep,
> Pulse nigh to pulse, and breath to breath,
> Where hushed awakenings are dear ...
> But I've a rendezvous with Death
> At midnight in some flaming town,
> When Spring trips north again this year,
> And I to my pledged word am true,
> I shall not fail that rendezvous.

After the analysis of the two poems the students have seen examples how to express war related emotions and are now set to start a transition from the text analysis to text creation, namely of their own poem. Instead of giving them a task of abstract expressive writing, they are now supposed to express themselves in a content-related way. However, the style of the poem itself—rhymes, lines, rhyme schemes etc.—is chosen and individually set by the students. The results are therefore very diverse, and while some poems resemble the starting points of the above named famous poems, others create something totally new based on the inspiration they received before.

One could, depending on the available time in the course, also allow the textual comparison of Seeger's letters, where he also describes the experience of a battle. A part of one letter to his mother on 25 October 1917 (Alan Seeger to his mother, October 25, 1917, in Alan Seeger, 1917: 164–173) is be quoted here in order to provide another text example for the description of a battle, in this specific case a battle in Champagne:

> The cannonade was pretty violent all that night, as it had been for several days previous, but toward dawn it reached an intensity unimaginable to anyone who has not seen a modern battle. A little before 9.15 [am] the fire lessened suddenly and the crackle of the fusillade between the reports of the cannon told us that the first wave of assault had left and the attack begun. At the same time we received the order to advance. The German artillery had now begun to open upon us in earnest. Amid the most infernal roar of every kind of firearms and through and atmosphere heavy with dust and smoke, we marched up ... At shallow places and over breaches that shells had made in the bank we caught momentary glimpses of the blue lines sweeping up the hillside or silhouetted on the crest where they poured into the German trenches. ... we crossed the open space between the lines, over barbed wire ... and over the German trench, knocked to pieces and filled with their dead. (Ibid., 165–166)

The students can now compare both text forms and discuss styles as well as advantages or disadvantages from a reader's perspective. However, the eventual target is to get them to write poetry, and the texts are solely supportive materials that help to grasp a sense of what it meant to be in a trench during the Great War.

Usually, in my experiences, the male students need a bit longer to embrace the idea of creating poetry. This may be the result of pre-established notions of masculinity and stereotypical concepts of gender roles and proclivities. However, once they overcome their initial resistance, the results are positve. In general, while students are skeptical at the beginning of the poem session in the classroom, they find it quite interesting in the end. With regard to the made experiences the analysis of a lyrical text with the aim to produce one's own written evidence, based on content the students received during the last few sessions can be valuable in many ways:

1. The instructor will reach all students, especially those who are usually bored by analytical or heavy source oriented sessions.
2. The instructor provides a more creative approach to a historical topic.
3. The experience of writing on their own does not only strengthen the memorization with regard to the topic—something one could observe in later essays as well—but it
4. Also strengthens the writing and language skills of the students.

However, there are some problems as well, which need to be taken into consideration, and prevented if possible, when dealing with expressive content writing in history courses:

1. The poem will not replace the historical experience itself, but at least provide an emotional approach.
2. The student has to be reminded that their work is related to a historical event to make sure that the boundary between imagination and history is not erased.
3. The method needs sufficient preparation. That means that one has to plan such a session in advance to integrate it into a topical block of the schedule.
4. Not all topics are suitable, as most of the students will need an existing text as an example with which to start.

4   Pilot Study

Having dealt with these experiences during my HIS 112 classes (Modern Western Civilization), I began, due to the pilot study at Queensborough Community College eventually was funded by a CETL pedagogical challenge grant, to look for colleagues in the Humanities who would be willing to incorporate poetry into their classes. I was fortunate to be able to persuade Dr. Amy Traver (Sociology) and Dr. Shannon Kincaid (Philosophy) to join the project, and together we developed course plans and strategies to integrate poetry into our classes. In my case, I decided not to use a HIS 112 course, but to try another one, namely the HIS 133 course, i.e. Introduction to Modern East Asian Civilizations.

The students, during the course were asked to complete the following poetry-based assignments—in addition to other writing and reading assignments:
- To read the "Memoirs of Babur"[11] and to describe some of the impressions related to the Silk Road in a 16 line poem.
- To read chapter 8 (Chinggis Khan and the Mongol Conquests) of Christopher I. Beckwith's *Empires of the Silk Road* (2011) and to sum up the chapter in a four stanzas, of which each had to follow one of the four basic metric feet, i.e. Iamb, Trochee, Anapest, and Dactyl.
- To write a poem describing the Rape of Nanjing from a victim's, perpetrator's, or bystander's perspective.

In particular, the last assignment, which was related to a lecture on the Rape of Nanjing and the "comfort women" issue in East Asian history,[12] forced the students to emotionally engage with the text itself. After having watched Bill Guttentag's and Dan Sturman's documentary *Nanking* (2007), the students were able to visualize the suffering of those who lived through the Rape of Nanjing as well as the images of the war crimes committed between December 1937 and March 1938.[13] To illustrate this point, some of the students' poems are included below.[14]

Nanking Poem

> Have you ever faced such terror in your life?
> Well I have I still have horrible dreams till this day every night
> It is 1937 in Nanking, China a place which became full of pain and strife
> The Japanese who were ally to the Nazis air raided china with bombs for miles
> My family and I fled trying to escape and hide wondering how we would escape
> This trial or if we would live
> We found a place to hide but to no avail
> Because soon after they found us and Japanese soldier bullets rained like hail

They found us my mother urged for my sister and I to flee without her
so we
Would be safe
We left as my mother told us of course we didn't want to go
But my mom would do anything to protect us even give her own life
So in a rush my sister and I hurried away and my mother was unfortu-
nately killed
After that tragedy I felt ill seeing the blood spill out of my mother looking
back
A couple of days had passed and another tragedy had happened my sister
was
Taken and raped in front of me then stabbed repeatable as Japanese
soldiers
Forced me to watch as I begged them to stop and they left me there after
they
Were done I cried there as I looked at my sister dead on the floor bloody
Wondering when it would end
Have you ever faced such terror in your life?
Well I have I still have horrible dreams till this day every night
This is my story

Rape of Nanking

The tale of bloodshed that shook the entire city,
The tale of monsters and savages,
That won't be seen in any lectures or textbooks,
The injustice done to the women and people,
The time of dominance and brutality.

The Japanese troops were demons,
Raping women without shame,
And killing thousands of men without hearts,
Without kindness and peace.

It didn't matter if they were a rich or poor,
It didn't matter if they were high or low,
No matter, who they were,
They stripped them and killed them,
Without hearts and mercy.

For the Japanese this never happened,
For the entire world it laid deep down like a mystery,
No one ever lived to tell the tale,
Of the bad dream of the Nanjing city.

Untitled

Where has love and peace gone?
Japan overflows as China's people just hide or go,
Nowhere to go, but fight or die.
China became the biggest victim, yet no one would find the courage to save them.
A man whose heart was pure gold he saw so much hate yet still kept a smile upon his face to Bandage up the broken pain.
Young men and women were killed, either raped or seen as soldiers escaping.
These people looked forward to time, as if that was their own hope for surviving such crimes.
These soldiers did not know otherwise, but power took over and made them blind and unwise.
Safety zones were comfort zones to those whom had no home.
Brutal deaths increased and piled up like mountains.
On the streets, in front of children, no mercy no sorrow.
As time passed, japan and China talked it out,
But how could you be sorry?
When you can't bring back the light that japan had once burnt out.
Tears flowing on a family member's face, how can you apologize, when all you have done is take Their sister's life and make it disappear.
Dark clouds once stayed over China, but as peace stood by and Japan's power weakened,
Sunshine decided to burst out, and
China was freed once again.

While the topic of the Rape of Nanjing usually causes the highest level of student interaction, I personally had the feeling that poetry provided the students with a more than suitable way to express deeper emotional levels related to the topic. However, besides these observations, the pilot study, of course, was also intended to check for possible grade changes.

One has to emphasize here that the number of students in the poetry based course and the control group (n=25) was rather small, especially since not all students filled out the IRB consent forms. Therefore, the statistically measurable outcome was rather limited. While the class, which had to deal with the poetry assignments, achieved an average grade of B (85.3) the control group was only slightly below that, but also achieved an average B grade (84.45). It could, however, be observed, that the grade gap between the A and D students, which existed in the control group, did not appear in the poetry-based class, in which more students were able to achieve solid B grades. It is just an assumption that would have to be proven in further studies with larger groups[15]—maybe a college-wide study—to see if there is any grade effect that is caused by the use of poetry in the classroom.

Nevertheless, in the poetry-based course, the intensity of discussions and the increased interest of students in the subject were visible outcomes within the pilot study. Whether the approach is used in a single course session or over a whole semester, the use of poetry in the Humanities seems to be promising and provides an alternative, especially for historians, who have the possibility to use a different source format in the classroom from time to time as well.

5 Conclusion

Regardless of the mentioned problems, I think that the method of expressive content writing will enrich history classes and that poetry provides a very valuable source form for the classroom. Even if one cannot reach all students, especially since this specific text form might deter some students, the integration of interdisciplinary approaches stands to engage students who might get bored by a common teacher-centered education or classical text analysis. The method is, of course, not limited to poetry; it could also work with letters, newspaper articles, announcements etc., but the poem as a text form provides a particular emotional setting for the writing experience to be even more intensified by students producing their own poetry. The history professor or teacher consequently has sufficient options to integrate it as a diversified method of teaching the subject.

The analysis was so far, while mostly based on limited-trial experience, able to indicate that there is promise for the use of poetry in history courses. I was regularly impressed at how interested the students became in the topic by using poetry as a frame to express themselves and their interpretations of such an important historical events like the First World War or the Rape of Nanjing.

Notes

1   It is hard to overview all recent publications related to the First World War, but there are some major publications that should be mentioned here (Clark, 2014; Winter, 2014). For a specific US perspective see: Faulkner (2017).

2   On the advantage of eyewitness reports and oral testimony in teaching history see Phillips (2010: 114–118).
3   I would like to thank my fellow PIs, Drs. Amy Traver and Shannon Kincaid, both members of the Social Sciences Department at Queensborough Community College, for their willingness to participate in this pilot study.
4   One example for a useful World War I reader is Neiberg (2006). Another prominent source that is usually read in the classroom when the First World War and the situation of the soldiers in the trenches or on the battlefields are discussed is Jünger (2004).
5   As one example how an emotional discourse can be created by the use of poetry in the classroom see Sims and Lea (2008: 67–77).
6   For the transformation of texts see Rai (2012: 20).
7   For a possible approach for the assessment of student poems see Griswold (2006: 70–75).
8   The British publishing house Pen & Sword publishes the series Images of War. The single volumes related to World War I provide valuable materials that can be used in the classroom.
9   For a discussion of diversity and its role in the classroom see Terenzini, Cabrera, Colbeck, Bjorklund and Parente (2001).
10 On textual semiotics see Lotman (1988). For a more extent discussion of applied semiotics related to text analysis see Hébert (2011).
11 "The Memoirs of Babur." Accessed December 10, 2017. http://depts.washington.edu/silkroad/texts/babur/babur1.html
12 Dr. Margaret Stetz, Mae and Robert Carter Professor of Women's Studies and Professor of Humanities at the University of Delaware, also gave a guest lecture, "Reframing the 'Comfort Women' Issue: New Representations of an Old War Crime," for the students, which was held on Monday, December 12, 2016 at the CUNY Graduate Center. The lecture was part of the CUNY Academy's Lecture Series on Mass Violence and Genocide in Asia (2016–2017), which was organized by the author and Dr. Kenneth Pearl (History Department, Queensborough Community College).
13 On this issue see: Jacob (2017). A more detailed analysis of Japanese war crimes during the Second World War is provided in Jacob (2018).
14 Smaller language issues and typos have been adjusted. Student's writings are published with IRB permission, which was granted due.
15 While there is a "common read" initiative at Queensborough Community College, in which all disciplines integrate a specific book into their class, there might be space for a "common poetry" initiative in the future to gather more data.

References

Beckwith, Christopher I. (2011). *Empires of the silk road: A history of Central Eurasia from the bronze age to the present.* Princeton, NJ: Princeton University Press.

Clark, Christopher. (2014). *Sleepwalkers: How Europe went to war in 1914.* New York, NY: Harper Perennial.

Faulkner, Richard. (2017). *Pershing's crusaders.* Lawrence, KS: University of Kansas Press.

Griswold, Andrea. (2006). Assessment lists: One solution for evaluating student poetry. *The English Journal, 96*(1), 70–75.

Haas, Gerhard, Menzel, Wolfgang, & Spinner, Kaspar H. (1994). Handlungs- und produktionsorientierter Literaturunterricht. *Praxis Deutsch, 123,* 17–25.

Hébert, Louis. (2011). *Tools for text and image analysis: An introduction to applied semiotics.* Retrieved December 6, 2017, from http://www.signosemio.com/documents/Louis-Hebert-Tools-for-Texts-and-Images.pdf

Jacob, Frank. (2017). Banzai! and the others die—Japanese soldiers and collective violence during the second Sino-Japanese war (1937–1945). In Michael Pfeifer (Ed.), *Global lynching and collective violence: Asia, Africa, and the Middle East* (Vol. 1, pp. 78–102). Champaign, IL: Illinois University Press.

Jacob, Frank. (2018). *Japanese war crimes during world war II: Atrocity and the psychology of collective violence.* Santa Barbara, CA: Praeger.

Jünger, Ernst. (2004). *Storm of steel.* London: Penguin.

Kennan, George F. (1979). *The decline of Bismarck's European order: Franco-Russian relations, 1875–1890.* Princeton, NJ: Princeton University Press.

Lotman, Yu M. (1988). The semiotics of culture and the concept of a text. *Soviet Psychology, 26*(3), 52–58.

Mullally, Erin. (2013). Deadly retreat. *Archaeology, 66*(4), 40–42.

Neiberg, Michael S. (Ed.). (2006). *The world war I reader.* New York, NY: New York University Press.

Norris, Margot. (2005). Teaching world war I poetry: Comparatively. *College Literature, 32*(3), 136–153.

Phillips, Dan. (2010). What lies beneath the history of conflict? Using personal testimony for learning. *Oral History: Power and Protest, 38*(1), 114–118.

Rai, Lucy. (2012). Responding to emotion in practice-based writing. *Higher Education, 64*(2), 267–284.

Raisch, Herbert. (1998). Überlegungen zum handlungs- und produktionsorientierten Geschichtsunterricht. *Beihefter zu Praxis Geschichte, 5,* 30–36.

Rennell, Rony. (2014, August 3). Horror beyond imagination. *Daily Mail.* Retrieved December 6, 2017, from http://www.dailymail.co.uk/news/article-2715098/The-haunting-account-trenches-ll-read-brilliant-anthology-Birdsong-author-Sebastian-Faulks.html

Seeger, Alan. (1917). *Letters and diary of Alan Seeger*. New York, NY: Charles Scribner's Sons.

Sims, Erma Jean & Lea, Virginia. (2008). Transforming whiteness through poetry: Engaging the emotions and invoking the spirit. *Counterpoints, 321*, 67–77.

Terenzini, Patrick T., Cabrera, Alberto F., Colbeck, Carol L., Bjorklund, Stefani A., & Parente, John M. (2001). Racial and ethnic diversity in the classroom: Does it promote student learning? *The Journal of Higher Education, 72*(5), 509–531.

Waugh, Daniel C. (1999). *The memoirs of Babur.* Retrieved December 10, 2017, from http://depts.washington.edu/silkroad/texts/babur/babur1.html

Winter, Jay. (2014). *The cambridge history of the first world war* (Vol. 3). Cambridge: Cambridge University Press.

PART 5

Philosophy

∴

CHAPTER 9

Pedagogy in Verse
A Philosophical Approach to Poetry across the Curriculum

Shannon Kincaid

1 Introduction

What is the post-secondary pedagogical role of poetry outside Departments of English and Literature? Would requiring students to write and read poems as part of the assessment of student learning in courses across the disciplines have a meaningful impact on both qualitative (self-reported) satisfaction surveys, and a quantifiable positive impact on student performance?

More specifically, how might poetry improve student learning in an introductory ethics course? Would the class benefit from an increased emphasis on poetry as it relates to the course material? And perhaps most importantly, what is the relationship between philosophy, pedagogy, and poetry?

Philosophy and poetry have a complicated relationship. Some philosophers (perhaps most) seem to like poetry. But some do not. Plato (427–347 BC) did not like poetry very much: "[W]e have come to see that we must not take such poetry seriously as a serious thing that lays hold on truth, but that he who lends an ear to it must on his guard fearing for the polity in his soul …" (Plato, 1961: 608b). Actually, Plato hated poetry. He argued that it lacks adequate justification to be considered as a form of knowledge. According to Charles Griswold, in the *Republic*,

> Plato quotes bits of several obscure but furious polemics—presumably directed by poets against philosophers such as the accusation that the opponent is a "yelping bitch shrieking at her master" and "great in the empty eloquence of fools." Indeed, much of the final book of the *Republic* is an attack on poetry, and there is no question but that a quarrel between philosophy and poetry is a continuing theme throughout Plato's *corpus*. (Griswold, 2016)

Aristotle (384–322 BC) liked poetry. He wrote a whole book about it (*Poetics*), and he was fascinated by the combination of language and rhythm that defines/determines/directs the subjective content of poetry. Unlike Plato, he thought that sensory experience could give us knowledge. In *The Critique of Judgment* (Kant, 1987), Immanuel Kant (1724–1804) argued that poetry was the highest form of art, independent of the senses yet connected to them. Alfred North Whitehead (1861–1947), in his *Modes of Thought* (Whitehead, 1938) claimed that unlike prose, poetry (like music, drama, and dance) represents its subject as a living thing, not as a past event. Justus Buchler (1914–1991) went one step further, arguing that poetry produces knowledge of the world by fusing subjective description with intersubjective experience, and that it enhances our collective understanding of who we are, and how we connect with the universe.

"Knowledge" is typically understood as "justified true belief." Science gives us knowledge with empirical evidence. Philosophy gives us theories of knowledge by appealing to logic and warrant. But what does poetry "do?" How can it deepen our understanding of the world and our connection to it?

Kant attempted to answer this question by looking at the function and limits of language, and he made a distinction between propositions (sentences, phrases, etc.) that "describe" the world, and those that add to our knowledge of the world. This is Kant's (in)famous distinction between analytic and synthetic propositions, and his claim that analytic propositions are just definitions while synthetic propositions produce knowledge (think of the difference between dictionaries and encyclopedias). Kant argued that synthetic a posteriori propositions (science) actually add to our knowledge of the world. But how can one person's description of the world they experience produce a deeper understanding of the world we all experience?

Kant and Buchler had an answer to this question. They both argued that we all experience the same world (probably), that there are some basic categories of experience that might be universal, but that we all experience that world in different ways. Unlike the empiricist John Locke (1632–1704), who believed that experience was the passive reception of the sense data thrown at us by the objects of the world (Locke, 1996) they both argued that we actively structure our experience. Kant's experiential categories were universal, Buchler's not so much, but they agreed, along with Hume (sort of) (Hume, 1992), Whitehead, and Aristotle, that your perception of the world, if not determined, is at least shaped by the categories through which you perceive the world. Some of these categories might be universal to all of human experience (space/time, cause and effect, quantity), but others are learned (strike zones, style, taste). As Buchler argued, "Poetry may be divine madness, as Plato calls it—inventive deviation from the safely inertial side of human judgment. But it is not alone in this status. In its very uniqueness as a discipline, it is continuous with all the other disciplines that are possessed by query" (Buchler, 1974: 173).

In other words, poetry does more than just describe the world. It adds to our understanding of the world, it asks questions, and, like all forms of inquiry, attempts to answer them in its own way. And in this sense, poetry is a discipline that transcends all disciplines. But can the introduction of poetic expression have a positive impact on student learning in introductory philosophy classes?

2   Ethics and Poetry

The pedagogical experiment described below was based on the premise that a combination of the analytic/descriptive elements of language might help inform the synthetic/knowledge producing goals of higher education. The goal was moving beyond simply delivering content, but of helping our students move past mere memorization and towards a deeper understanding of the relationships between the diverse disciplines they are studying in college. In other words, can the introduction of poetry across the disciplines improve student learning outcomes?

Based on this question, the philosophy class selected for participation in the pilot study (PHI 130. Ethics: Theories of the Good Life. Fall Semester, 2016. Section D24. Tu/Th, 10:40–11.55, M 332) incorporated the following series of new assignments, readings, and assessment instruments into the course.

On the first day of class, students were given two informal writing assignments. The first was a two-page typewritten essay asking students to describe the principles and methods which guide their moral judgments. For the second assignment, students were asked to write a haiku about moral issues that affect them personally on blank paper in landscape orientation. Both assignments were due on the third class meeting.

In both classes, the responses to the first assignment were very similar, and there didn't seem to be an appreciable difference in the quality of the assignments between the two groups. Students mentioned things like "caring for others," "compassion," "making people happy," and "following the rules." Several students referred to their religious traditions as the foundation for their moral deliberations.

The haiku assignment in the experimental cohort yielded some very interesting results. The assignment was very specific, both in structure and presentation. And while some of the students completed the assignment in a haphazard way (some writing in verse, but not haiku; others obviously scratching out the assignment at the last minute), most of the students took it very seriously.

These students painstakingly used various font styles and sizes for the assignment (two of them wrote out the poem in calligraphy, with one of them using archival paper), and overall, the results were very good. Here are a few examples:

> Taking of a life
> Assisted suicide. They
> Suffer or they die

> My grades fell apart
> When my dad called me stupid
> I am not perfect

> What is a Woman Worth?
> Everything on this Earth
> When will they realize?

> Won't you be haunted?
> Killing innocent creatures
> For your indulgence

> Racial Equity
> Makes the world a better place
> Go! Make a statement

The next assignment was based on our class discussions concerning the relationships between Stoicism and Hedonism. As a class, we agreed that both philosophies are based on very different metaphysical premises (atomism vs. *Logos*), but that there was an interesting connection between the stoics and the hedonists: Neither one of them seek fame and fortune, nor do they fear death. The assignment consisted of a worksheet starting with Emily Bronte's "Riches I Hold in Light Esteem." It then asked students to write a poem (in longhand) describing the conversation between a hedonist and a stoic as they lay on their deathbeds. Students were encouraged to consider the concepts of *Logos*, atomism, happiness, pleasure, the absence of pain, anonymity, moderation, and the tension between emotion and reason in their verse. They were also asked to consider the works of Plato, Hume, Aristotle, and some of the other philosophers we discussed in class.

Most of the students obviously spent a great deal of time and effort on the assignment. Here are two examples:

"As I Lay Here"

As I lay here
Allowing myself to go if that's what they want
I have had my share here
And if I must go I will
I am happy for what its given me
Health, wealth, and happiness
But if says it's over then I must go
Just promise me this
My people will what was mine
So they can fulfill same as I
and when you say it's time for them
then let them pass on
With this pleasure I know you know
What you're doing
Do what you do best but don't
let it hurt

"P.O.C."

My lifetime in a colorless word
The screams of solitary flesh tones
I remember being in your mono-culture universe
A blemish on your delicate ears

The mask I dawn in your sphere
Is unreal
Shield my life from the lies I inhale
The truth is in the injustice we see
But hidden behind peach faced monsters on T.V.

Why must our culture drown in vain?
Rinsed and bleached, as we are the stains

> In their world, free of me and mine
> Barren domicile of the other kind.
>
> Can we speak about it?
> The whips
> The cracks
> The don't talk backs
> The crooked sidewalks, the broken tradition
> The refusal of your ears
> The sits and listens
> The pots
> The pans
> The clasping of hands
> As we pray for those better days
> Where you loosen the reigns
> Unlink the chains
> And let color bleed free in the sky

The next assignment was an in-class written reflection on Friedrich Nietzsche's "Parable of a Madman" (1882). A handout was distributed at the beginning of class, and the students were given thirty minutes to read the poem and identify the passages that affected them the most, and to explain why they selected those passages. They also had to answer the question, "Is Nietzsche's Madman crazy?" An adequate account of the diversity and depth of the responses to this assignment goes well beyond the limits of this essay. Some students argued that he was crazy for throwing the lamp, others said he was crazy but only because he was ahead of his time. Several students said that in any society, anyone who questions "popular belief negatively [is] ridiculed and even called crazy." Other students argued that he was not crazy: "There are other things that may be considered crazy, but in this case of searching for answers, he is just being human."

3   Assessment

Each exam included a short answer question dealing with one of the central themes of the assigned poems. The first exam contained a required question of both cohorts (students are given five short answer questions, of which they are to choose four to answer). On the midterm, the required question asked students to discuss the relationships between the metaphysical assumptions of stoicism and hedonism, and the differences and similarities between their respective accounts of "the good life."

There was no statistical difference in the grades received by the two cohorts on this question. The grading criteria was based on the adequacy of the description of the metaphysical differences between the two positions, and the similarities between them. In the experimental group, the answers focused exclusively on the fear of dying. The control group was more diverse in its responses, referring to the hedonist conception of happiness as the mere absence of pain and the stoic demand that we must accept our fate in a sentient universe that we cannot understand.

On the final exam, both groups were given a mandatory short answer question asking what Nietzsche meant when he said that "God is dead." Again, both groups showed little difference in their overall scores on the question. The experimental cohort often referred to the poem, but both groups demonstrated a good understanding of Nietzsche' rejection of traditional moral codes, and his rejection of "slave" morality.

Overall, there was no statistically significant difference in the final grades received by both cohorts. Student evaluations in both classes were very positive. However, there was significant evidence of increased student satisfaction with the class among those who came into the semester with an appreciation of poetry, and there were many students who seemed to leave the course with a newfound respect and appreciation for poetic expression. While not required to do so, many students incorporated poetry into their formal term papers, and several referred to poetic works in the essays on the final exam.

The final assessment tool for the project consisted of a four question worksheet based on the following four questions:

— Is ethical decision-making more akin to poetry or mathematics?
— Did our use of poetry have any impact on your comprehension of the course materials, and did it help you develop your writing skills?
— Did our use of poetry have any effect on your understanding of ethics?
— Would you recommend a poetry-based course format to a fellow student of friend? Why or why not?

The first question was designed to gauge the class's reflections on the tension between objectivity and subjectivity in ethical decision-making. The responses were evenly divided. Those that argued that ethics is more aligned with mathematics said ethics involved:

— specific calculations,
— complexity,
— thinking about things in more than one way,

- it involves logic in a way poetry does not, and
- being ethical is strategic and logical, whereas poetry is neither.

Students that argued that ethical-decision making is poetic said that ethics "is a more emotion-based process and this is more akin to poetry than mathematics," "[P]oetry, because ethics is not something you can put a number on but something more internal and something like poetry is more 'feeling,'" and finally, "Originally, I might have said mathematics because I would have associated ethics with logic and reasoning and would have to say that it is similar to math. However, after studying Hume, I would have [to] say poetry because he would argue that ethics derives from emotions which I would associate with poetry."

On the second question regarding the impact of the use of poetry on comprehension of the course materials and an improvement in writing skills, the responses were mixed.

- Poetry helped me think of ethical issues in a creative way,
- It helped me think in different ways and connect to different ideas,
- It helped me to better apply different terms and use of concepts in my everyday writing,
- For me, not really because I have trouble personally with interpreting poetry, but it did help in the sense of being able to look at the material from a different perspective.

While most students responded positively to the inclusion of poetry into the course material, several students disagreed with the project. "In some ways [the incorporation of poetry into the curriculum] was a barrier, but it did give me a chance to be creative," "Actually, not really. I'd actually prefer to not have poetry involved with this class," "I hate poetry," and "I think ethics and poetry are two separate beautiful faculties." However, almost all students agreed that the assignment involving Nietzsche's "Parable of a Madman" was very helpful in understanding the basic tenets of ethical subjectivism. "The poem not only helped me remember Nietzsche's theory but it made the theory more comprehensive."

Finally, the last question ("Would you recommend a poetry-based course format to a fellow student or friend?") resulted in a diversity of responses.

- No, it didn't make much of a difference, [but] if a friend enjoys poetry, I would recommend it,
- Probably not, a regular ethics class would have been great,

- I would. I don't think poetry is for everyone, but should stay for those that it would benefit. I think it can also help those who aren't usually exposed to poetry,
- Yes, everyone should attempt to understand the unique abstract concepts of poetry [and] philosophy,
- Yes, it's not completely as bad as I expected as I thought it would be when first introduced, and
- I would highly recommend a poetry based course. I believe it cultivates language skills, which is declining art form. In order to keep language alive, [poetry] should be included in more classes.

In summary, while there was no measurable difference in the quantitative performance of the students in each cohort, it was readily apparent that the inclusion of at least some poetry in the curriculum was beneficial to the class regarding how their emotions relate to their attempts to employ "reason" in their ethical decision-making. Also, based on the pilot study, courses like "Sociology/History/Philosophy for Poets" might be considered. Not all students respond positively to poetic content, but for those that do, it makes a significant difference in their appreciation for the material.

Acknowledgments

I must first thank Drs. Jacob and Traver for initiating this project, and Dr. Kathleen Landy, director of QCC's Center on Excellence in Teaching and Learning, for her support. On a personal note, this pedagogical experiment has had a tremendous impact on my teaching and my appreciation of poetry. It has been a tremendous amount of work, but it has really informed my teaching, it seems to have been a very positive experience for my students, and I think all of us came away from the project with a newfound appreciation for poetic expression, and its applicability across the disciplines.

References

Buchler, Justus. (1974). *In the main of light: On the concept of poetry.* New York, NY: Oxford University Press.

Griswold, Charles L. (2016). Plato on rhetoric and poetry. In Edward N. Zalta (*Ed.*), *The Stanford encyclopedia of philosophy*. Stanford, CA: Metaphysics Research Lab. Retrieved November 29, 2017, from https://plato.stanford.edu/archives/fall2016/entries/plato-rhetoric/

Hume, David. (1992). *An inquiry concerning human understanding.* Indianapolis, IN: Hackett.

Kant, Immanuel. (1987). *A critique of judgment* (Werner S. Pluhar, Trans.). Indianapolis, IN: Hackett.

Locke, John. (1996). *An essay concerniwng human understanding.* Indianapolis, IN: Hackett.

Plato. (1961). *Republic, in collected works of Plato* (Paul Shorey, Trans., Edith Hamilton & Huntington Cairns, Eds.). Princeton, NJ: Princeton University Press.

Whitehead, Alfred North. (1938). *Modes of thought.* New York, NY: Macmillian.

CHAPTER 10

Empowering Poetic Defiance
Baudelaire, Kant and Poetic Agency in the Classroom

Joshua M. Hall

Many strategies for incorporating poetry into non-poetry classes, especially outside of English and associated disciplines, appear to make poetry subservient and secondary in relation to the prose content of the course. The poet under consideration becomes a kind of involuntary servant to one or more prose authors, forced to "speak only when spoken to," and effectively prevented from challenging the ideas of the course's prose writers, and thereby the instructor. This was my experience in virtually every philosophy course that I took, as an undergraduate and graduate student, into which poetry was incorporated, at both the level of the primary texts and also the level of the teaching of those texts. For example, in a course dedicated to Plato (423–348 BCE), we read Plato using Homer in this way, and this using was affirmed by the professor (Plato, 1986). The same is true for Hegel's (1770–1831) use of the tragic poet Sophocles' *Antigone*, and for Martin Heidegger's (1889–1976) use of the poet Hölderlin (1770–1843), in the way that such usage was taught to me (Hegel, 1977; Heidegger, 2001). In each case, the philosopher makes a claim, quotes a poet (usually out of context), and interprets the quote as supporting the original claim.

The problem with this strategy is that the prose theorists are seeking to buttress the legitimacy of their analyses by claiming to know that poetic theorists would agree with them (based on what are often highly selective and idiosyncratic interpretations of lines of their poetry). Put schematically, if a theorist A, in an attempt to persuade a reader B of the truth of a claim X, invokes the authority of a poet C, then that invocation is illegitimate unless A has good reason to believe that C would agree with X. Otherwise, A is misrepresenting C. Moreover, since A is a prose theorist while C is a poet, and since this type of misrepresentation is prevalent both historically and today, it has exacerbated the undermining of the intellectual authority of poetry and poets per se in an academic classroom setting. The beginning of this academic trend, however, I locate in the work of Immanuel Kant (1724–1804), to whom I will return at length below.

Perhaps some conscientious readers have become concerned, at this point, that any use of poetry in their classrooms would be too risky, too likely to be complicit in the kind of misrepresentation and undermining I am describing, and that they should therefore abandon the practice entirely. On the contrary, I would argue that the long history of this problem is the very reason why it is so important for teachers to incorporate poetry in a more respectful way—to help reverse some of this damage, and facilitate an academic environment more respectful of the intellectual powers of poetry. Moreover, the mistakes one might make in the process are not irredeemable, and can even function as learning experiences for both the teacher and the students. The most important thing is to make a concerted effort to create spaces in a course where poets, in their different voices, can be heard.

Toward that end, in this chapter, I will suggest an alternate approach for faculty which recognizes and facilitates the agency of poets and poetry per se, which I term "empowering poetic defiance." In brief, this approach consists of the following four steps:

1. challenge one's own poetic self-loathing
2. position the course's poetry's content to challenge the course's non-poetic contents
3. position the course's poetry's forms to challenge one's class's non-poetic forms
4. comport oneself as interlocutor toward the poets in one's course on the strategic assumption that they are the intellectual equals of both oneself and of the prose theorists in the course.

My first section will elaborate on these four steps, drawing on my early experiences as a poet studying poetry in philosophy courses, and my later teaching experiences, with an emphasis on a section of Introduction to Philosophy that I taught at Vanderbilt University in the fall of 2009, the theme of which was the relationship between philosophy and poetry, and the required readings for which were half poetry and half prose philosophy, namely *The Book of Ecclesiastes*, Plato's *Ion*, Boethius' (480–525 CE) *The Consolation of Philosophy*, Christine de Pizan's (1364–1430 CE) *Selected Writings*, Shakespeare's (1564–1616) *The Tempest*, Condillac's (1714–1780) *Essay on the Origin of Human Language*, Schiller's (1759–1805) *On the Aesthetic Education of Man*, Nietzsche's (1844–1900) *The Gay Science*, Dewey's (1859–1952) *Experience and Nature*, and Wole Soyinka's (1934) *Death and the King's Horseman* (Boethius, 2008; Bonnot de Condillac, 2001; Coogan, 2007; Nietzsche, 2000; Plato, 1925; Schiller, 2004; Shakespeare, 2003; Soyinka, 2002). I will also refer to two sections of Introduction to Philosophy that I currently teach at CUNY Queensborough, entitled "The Psyche and the Soul," and "Philosophy as Demonology." In the former, we read Sufi poetry by Rumi (1207–1273) and Hafiz (1315–1390), and poetry composed by the Neo-Confucian philosopher Wang Yangming (1472–1529); in the latter, we read a verse translation of the poetry of the *Bhagavad-Gita*, poems from Nietzsche's *The Gay Science*; and in both, we read poems from Gloria Anzaldúa's (1942–2004) *Borderlands/La Frontera* (*The Bhagavad-Gita*, 1986; also see: Anzaldúa, 2012). Since Vanderbilt is a predominantly white, upper-SES, private, Research 1 university, and CUNY Queensborough is a racially diverse, lower-SES, public community college, the similarity of the results at both schools suggests to me a wide scope of applications for this method.

My second section will then test the effectiveness of this defiant method by making explicit a challenge from one of the most influential modern poets, Baudelaire, to the most influential modern philosopher, Kant. The latter theorist, arguably the least poetic canonical Western philosopher, is largely responsible for the overall structure of the modern university, with its strict disciplinary boundaries and its dichotomous opposition between religion (including poetry) and the sciences.[1] And Charles Baudelaire (1844–1866) is the posterchild for poetic decadence and irresponsibility, rejecting the kind of institutionalized knowledge and legitimacy that give the modern university its power. In other words, it is in this second section that I will try to practice what I am preaching, enabling a poet to criticize a philosopher who is in many ways the source of the problem that this new method is attempting to resolve. In the course of this effort, I will also make an argument for my fellow educators who teach Kant to seriously consider including a response to him from Baudelaire.

1   Four Steps to Poetic Defiance

I begin, as every theoretical dance should, with step one. The Western tradition, beginning with Plato's exile of the dramatic poets from the *Republic*, is partially defined by a millennia-long history of self-loathing poets, who disavow their poetic identity and don the mask of prose scholar instead. Plato himself was a tragic poet before meeting Socrates, after which he burned all his poems. Yet at Plato's death, a copy of Sappho's lyric poetry was discovered under his pillow.[2] Even as great and committed a poet as John Milton claimed, in the epilogue to his 1645 *Poems*, to have outgrown his own poetry (which he calls "vain trophies of my idleness") thanks to Plato's "Academy's Socratic streams" (Milton, 2008: 123). This poetic self-loathing can also be detected, as I will discuss below, in Baudelaire, despite his status as perhaps the greatest poet in French history.

For my own humbler part, having written poetry for years before I began to study philosophy, I was heartbroken to learn, as an undergraduate, of Plato's apparent contempt for the poets, and hurt by my colleagues and mentors' dismissiveness toward philosophers writing poetry. Though I had written seriously and published since undergrad days, I wrote very little poetry during my seven years of grad school in philosophy. This was not only due to the extreme workload, and stress, both of which were actually worse for me during my subsequent three years of adjunct teaching (at three schools simultaneously). Yet I still produced much more poetry as an adjunct than during grad school. I attribute the latter decreased output to a pervasive ambiance of contempt in both of my graduate programs toward philosophers writing poetry. This, despite many of my professors and peers claiming, with apparent sincerity, to have a high regard for poets and poetry. Their objection, I eventually concluded, was the blurring of boundaries between philosophy and poetry, perceived as properly divided along the Kantian lines of concepts versus sensations. From this perspective, since I had enrolled in a Ph.D. in Philosophy program, I had decided in favor of concepts, and thus should not waste my creative intellectual energies on the sensations to which philosophy reduces poetry. In short, I now believe I was then experiencing a period of poetic self-loathing. To resist these pressures, I devoted my first dissertation to trying to rise to Plato's challenge, in the *Republic*, and be the poet who someday proves the poets worthy of re-admittance to his imaginary polis.

Since virtually everyone has composed poetry, at least during childhood, instructors of prose-dominated courses should do some soul-searching before introducing poetry into those courses, and ask whether they, too, have internalized this contempt for theorists drawn to verse. Moreover, one should strategically assume that one or more of one's students are in a similar position, namely poets who might be struggling with their own poetic self-loathing as they engage in a formal classroom dedicated to prose theory. I have had numerous students over the years who were openly relieved and excited when they realized that we would be reading poetry, that they could choose to write their required essays on poems instead of prose texts, and that they were allowed (even encouraged) to use poetic strategies (including metaphors) in their analyses of poetic and prose texts. For example, one of the student papers form the "poetry and philosophy" Intro course was written on a Bible verse from the Apocryphal Book of Ecclesiastes (which also allowed that student to explore a sacred text from his religious tradition in a philosophical and poetic context).

The second step in empowering poetic defiance involves an attempt to include, in the course's poetic content, poetry which does not merely confirm the claims and perspectives already represented by the course's prose content. In all of my courses, for example, I encourage the students to use each primary historical text to critique all of the others, such as when they read poems by Nietzsche mocking Descartes' (1596–1650) conception of the human being as an essentially rational subject, or Sufi poetry that challenges the apparent Muslim orthodoxy in the work of Abu Nasr Alfarabi (970–943). Although one might object that such a strategy is unrealistically demanding for most instructors who are not well-versed in poetry, locating such moments of poetic undermining is actually easy. One merely needs to perform a basic search, on a literary database such as Project MUSE, for the poet and prose writers' names. Perhaps the real obstacle is something like the instructor's unconscious attempt to prevent the poetic text from doing anything more than buttressing the legitimacy or persuasiveness of a given prose text. That is, if the instructor is unfamiliar with a poetic writer's divergence from a given prose writer, they may prefer not to know, and merely highlight any apparent convergence between the two.

Put differently, this second step enables the propositional content of the poetry (i.e. that in the poet's writing which can be translated or paraphrased into prose) to enter a conflictual dialogue with the prose content of the course. The difficulty here lies in being willing and able to treat poets' and prose theorists' claims as applying to the same world (in an ontological sense), or the same reality. The dominant approach in theoretical circles, by contrast, seems to assume that poetic writings map almost exclusively to imaginary and emotional arenas, while assuming that prose philosophical writings map onto an arena inclusive of the actual and rational. Most influential, in this regard, is the late-nineteenth century and early-twentieth century philosophical school of logical positivism, which argues that any sentence which cannot be empirically verified (like the sentences used in science) has no relationship to truth, and instead concerns either emotions (like the sentences in ethical discourse and literature) or is completely meaningless (like the sentences in metaphysical texts) (Ayer, 1952). In short, poetry is fictive and affective, while only prose can be real and cognitive.

The pervasiveness of this perspective is evident in the biggest challenge I face in this second step, namely my students' initial suspicion and incredulity. At both Vanderbilt and CUNY Queensborough, my students frequently questioned my choice to include poetic texts, and occasionally challenged me as to whether they constituted philosophy. I am usually able to persuade them, for the most part, by the end of the course, having explained that we will simply proceed from the strategic assumption that the poets and the prose philosophers are writing of shared phenomena in a shared world. Most helpful in this regard are my identification of rappers and hip-hop artists as poets, after which I ask the students if they consider those artists to be thinkers, truth-tellers, and seekers of wisdom. In other words, since they are unwilling to disqualify the poets whom they already love, they are usually willing to give the poets I am introducing to them the benefit of the doubt (which is all that poets worth their salt ever need, but which they rarely receive).

Where the second step empowers poetry to problematize the *content* of the prose writings featured in a course, the third step involves problematizing the *form* of the prose writings (and also, by implication, the prose-based methodologies of the course's academic discipline). This third step in empowering poetic defiance attempts to feature poetry that emphasizes—contra much prose scholarship and research—formal features characteristic of poetry contra prose. Important examples here include emotionally-charged language and rhetoric, first-person vantage points, and a willingness and ability to simultaneously affirm two or more claims that stand in logical tension or even contradiction. So intense are the effects of these formal characteristics of poetry that they often distract prose interpreters from realizing a poet and prose writer are even discussing the same content. As I will discuss below, this is frequently the case for Baudelaire and Kant, including in their shared emphasis on ethical and moral crises.

In other words, this third step attends to the formal dimensions of poetry, including the mathematics involved in traditional (non-prose) lyric poetry. One insight from this attentiveness is that poetry is both capable of much greater formal precision (to the point of counting and measuring each syllable in each poem), while also being much more flexible, in that it can disguise its poetic intent and craft in what appear to be mere prose paragraphs and short stories. Put differently, one can posit a continuum of formality/rigidity that ranges from formal metrical poetry (including traditional sonnets and haiku) to prose poetry, in the middle of which continuum conventional prose is both more and less formal/rigid than different types of poetry—lying in the boring middle, surrounded by mathematically precise metrical verse and wildly creative prose poetry.

Regarding the latter, moreover, it can tap into the considerable powers of articulation and expression unique to narrative fiction, whereas almost all philosophers writing in prose deny themselves the resources of this genre. Put simply, prose poetry tells stories, and openly, while prose maintains the pretense of not doing so. Examples of this storytelling power in my classes include the civil war narrative of the *Gita*, Shakespeare and Soyinka's dramatic narratives, and what Anzaldúa calls *"auto-historia,"* a genre-blending of autobiography, fiction and poetry. Against this powerful background, the prose philosophy appears to many students to be needlessly self-limiting and off-putting.

The fourth step, finally, is the organic result of having taken the first three. It should be emphasized that this step does not require it to be the case that poets in general, or a given poet in the course, are in fact intellectually equal to prose theorists, or a given prose theorist in the course. Instead, it merely proceeds on the strategic assumption that this is the case, to maximize respect and hermeneutic openness (consonant with the vision articulated in the contemporary French philosopher Jacques Rancière's famous pedagogical study, *The Ignorant Schoolmaster*) (Rancière, 1991). To treat a poet as intellectual equal to a prose writer, in this sense, presupposes (1) refraining from projecting one's own intellectual insecurities onto the poet, as an unconscious excuse to keep the poet from even joining the conversation to begin with, (2) giving a fair hearing to even those claims by the poet which challenge the central premises and assumptions of prose-dominated debates, and (3) maintaining hermeneutic openness and charity towards characteristically poetic forms of discourse.

Achieving and sustaining this egalitarian comportment toward a given poet is more difficult to the degree that the following traits tend to be attributed to the poet (corresponding to the first three steps of this method, respectively): (1) a hostility to theory per se, (2) a predilection for stances that are (currently) unpopular in prose-dominated theoretical circles, and (3) a valorization of phenomena such as affect, first-personness, and illogic. In this light, the maximally egalitarian non-poetry instructor would be willing and able to incorporate into prose-dominated courses even a poet regarded as antitheoretical, antiestablishment, and/or antilogical. It was in part to illustrate this point that I chose to focus in my second section on Baudelaire, maximally defiant, quintessentially poetic, and taking aim at Kant, one of the least egalitarian prose theorists, in respect of the hierarchy of poetry and prose.

Put differently, the fourth step is a refusal to dismiss poets qua thinkers—a refusal to pretend that one has no obligation, as an interpreter of philosophy, to attend to its dialogues with poetry. There is much at stake in this type of decision, both intellectually and professionally, for present-day instructors of prose-dominated courses. Because poets often question, mock and eviscerate academic theorists' deepest assumptions, and explore phenomena that continue to be frowned upon in most academic theoretical circles, wherein instructors seek employment, tenure, and advancement (not to mention collegial respect and community). The obligation, and the attendant risk, are real. Sometimes this can even happen with the oeuvre of a single author. In Wang Yangming's work, for example, while his prose tends to condemn Daoism and Buddhism as inherently self-centered and politically quietest, his poetry draws freely on and affirms themes and claims from both Daoism and Buddhism (Ivanhoe, 2009).[3] This then presents the opportunity for us to discuss the possibility that Wang's prose condemnations might have been more partial, and indeed strategic, than they appear on the surface.

In short, to practice this method of empowering poetic defiance, we as instructors in prose-dominated courses must be willing to empower ourselves, and to seek empowerment from likeminded others, in order to practice some significant defiance of our own. If we do not wish the invaluable differences and singularities of these rebellious poetic voices, views, and perspectives to pass from our world, then we must be willing to risk performing their rebelliousness, rather than just admiring that rebellion from the safety of our academic conformism. In other words, we should be as brave as the poets who challenge the philosophers of their own era, by invoking the poets of our own era who are challenging us.

But even if this is desirable, one might well ask what this looks like, concretely, and how the instructor of a prose-dominated course might get it done. To that end, I now turn to the second section of my chapter, which constitutes an extended example of such defiance, based on the deliberately defiant text I wrote for one of my two Comprehensive Examination questions as a Ph.D. student in philosophy. I was aware at the time that producing such a text might endanger my progress toward my doctorate, but I was also concerned that if I merely produced the kind of text that my examination committee was expecting, I would be taking another step in the direction of poetic deference. One of the names that loomed largest in that regard—as a prosaic obstacle to overcoming my own poetic self-loathing, using poetry to challenge the content and form of my philosophy course texts and professors, and comporting myself toward poets as the intellectual equals of philosophers—was Immanuel Kant. But I was determined to challenge him, and his representatives on the examination committee, by confronting his work with that of one poetic thinker whose poetic swagger did not seem at all welcome at the philosophical table.

2   Baudelairean Boredom Contra Kantian Critique

As I mentioned above, I chose to focus on Kant here in part because he arguably represents a major source and justification for the problem that this new method attempts to solve. And as I mentioned at the end of my first section, I also chose him in part because it was through struggling with his texts that I learned to practice poetic defiance myself, and much later managed to articulate that defiance as an explicit pedagogical method. Even if that were not the case, however, the most important part of the analysis that follows would remain, its force intact. To wit, I am attempting to demonstrate concretely what it looks like to read a prose theorist in juxtaposition with a poetic theorist, which reading can both precede and accompany the teaching of the theorists in a lower-level, undergraduate introductory philosophy course. Though I have not yet had the opportunity to teach Kant's theoretical philosophy, if I did I would certainly utilize the materials and interpretations in this section. And I have offered similar interpretations of similar texts in numerous introductory courses at multiple colleges, in each case following the same basic approach. I begin by assigning a text, which we discuss in a circular formation during our next class meeting, and then at the third class meeting I present to my students, in outline form, some interpretive points of my own regarding that text, which is then folded back into our subsequent discussions of that texts and the subsequent text for the course. In what follows, I will offer specific examples of how one might incorporate such interpretations into a prose-dominated classroom setting.

Returning to the singular case of Kant, it would not be unreasonable to claim that he almost singlehandedly inaugurates intellectual modernity, by transforming philosophy into the absolute Critic, the central responsibility of whom is the segregation of religion (including religious poetry) from science. So great is his influence that, even though my chosen historical era for the Comprehensive Examination was the nineteenth century, the question/prompt written by my committee for that exam focused on Kant. The prompt read as follows: "Although he lived in the eighteenth century, did the nineteenth century truly belong to Kant?" Although I continue to have enormous respect for my three committee members who chose and affirmed this prompt, my first reaction to it was indignance. Was it not already problematic enough, I asked myself, that one prose writer is widely regarded as the dominant force of his entire century? Must we also concede to him the next hundred years, too, extending his discursive empire so far past his own grave?

I knew that the expected, "correct" answer was "yes," because almost every philosopher from the nineteenth century who is currently taken seriously either falls into the Kant-based school of German Idealism (including Fichte, Schelling, Schopenhauer and Hegel) or the anti-Kantian, anti-Idealist precursors to existentialism (namely Kierkegaard and Nietzsche). The problem is that framing the issue this way excluded the most important poetic philosophers of the nineteenth century, including the American Transcendentalists (Emerson and Thoreau), the British Romanticists (including Coleridge, Shelley, Byron and Keats) and the French Symbolists (including Baudelaire, Mallarmé, and Rimbaud).

Attempting to defy what I saw as an institutionalized exclusion of the poets, I chose to deconstruct the concept of "belonging," in part by exploring its technical meaning in the field of mathematics, and specifically set theory (My choice of mathematical discourse was not arbitrary, however, because

Kant's influence on mathematics is actually almost as great as on philosophy, to which point I will return shortly). This deconstructive decision also illustrates an additional strategy for empowering poetic defiance, namely to reframe the subject at hand, by exploring the linguistic and rhetorical features of the subject, and being willing to pivot to a marginalized area (in this case mathematics) to utilize that area as the third term in a triangulation among it, the prose theorist, and a poet. In this case, for example, neither Kant nor Baudelaire are most famous for their relationship to mathematics, and it is the strong suit of neither, and yet perhaps for that reason it offered a kind of neutral terrain on which to explore a possible engagement and interrogation between the two thinkers.

As exploited (in every sense of the word) by the contemporary French philosopher Alain Badiou, "belonging" in set theory signifies that something is a member of a set. For example, the number 3 is a member of the set of whole numbers, and of the set of odd numbers (among an infinity of other actual and possible sets). This concept of belonging stands in contrast to the set theory concept of "inclusion," which signifies that one set belongs to another set. For example, the set of whole numbers is included in the set of integers. For Badiou, belonging corresponds to his concept of "presentation," while inclusion corresponds to his concept of "representation" (Badiou, 2007: 99). When something is represented, in Badiou's sense, that thing is presented as belonging; whereas when something belongs, it may not be also represented (i.e., presented *as* belonging). For example, the number 40,000,000 belongs to the set of whole numbers, but it is not often explicitly acknowledged as belonging to that set.

In this set theoretical mathematical sense, I am claiming that Baudelaire is the nineteenth-century writer who "belongs" to Kant's intellectual arena, while not being "included" therein, in that Baudelaire is not recognized and presented as occupying his actual location in Kant's orbit. This recourse to Badiou also illustrates yet another strategy for empowering poetic defiance, namely to consider the work of a later theorist who might have interests and research in a given pair of philosopher and poet. In his case, Badiou has an affinity for French Symbolists (though his favorite appears to be Mallarmé rather than Baudelaire) (Badiou, 2005).

To get a sense of part of what Kant meant to nineteenth-century thinkers such as Baudelaire, picture a guidebook, a how-to manual, on two of the oldest, commonest and most ineradicable of human activities. This guidebook, moreover, is so complex, so intimidating and so awkwardly written, that it has the following effects on its considerable audience: (1) many give up the first activity altogether, (2) many more believe they have given it up, but continue to engage in it, in a kind of Freudian denial, and (3) most of those who do continue the activity, willfully and consciously, are filled with guilt, shame and despair. Moreover, even the guidebook's author never manages, and perhaps for the same reasons as his readers, to complete his own contribution to this endeavor, after having published his preliminary book on method. We know, however, from that book on method, that the author did in fact have a tentative title for his contribution, namely *Metaphysics of Nature* (Kant, 1929: 14).

This description is incomplete, however, in that it considers only the first of the two activities revolutionized by this guidebook, namely metaphysics, which is the only concern for most prose philosophers. The second activity, mathematics, is naturally even more important for those working in the medium that is the marriage of philosophy and mathematics, especially by way of music, namely lyric poetry. This additional audience, the poet-philosophers (who are customarily referred to by only the first part of their name), must therefore also deal with Kant's first *Critique*'s treatment of mathematics. In the latter, Kant sets mathematics on roughly as unprecedented and unwanted a path as that on which he set metaphysics. The contemporary philosophy of mathematics terms this path "constructivism." In a nutshell, Kant argues that the same "Reason" which discovers the truths of philosophy actually creates mathematical truths, and that these mathematical truths, upon creation, become part of the fabric of the inter-subjective world of appearances.[4]

Thus, the metaphysicians, who historically have almost always insisted on creating, after Kant are essentially rendered infertile. And the mathematicians—who for the most part, if given to metaphysical speculation at all, have considered themselves discoverers of truth—after Kant are transformed into magicians. More specifically, in a claim more counterintuitive even than any in his first *Critique*, Kant elsewhere defines the mathematicians. "Mathematics," he writes, "is pure poetry" (Kant, 1993: 139). For a poet concerned with the subject matter of metaphysics, and there is arguably no other kind, the above information would have to be bewildering, perhaps even more so than for the prose philosophers. If taken seriously, it would entail a diremption for the poet into the strange psychic bedfellows of infertile metaphysician and fabricating mathematician, since the former supplies the content of lyric poetry, while the latter supplies its form.

Taking one last imaginative step, if one were to picture a poet after Kant, lingering with the tension of these claims long enough to produce a poetic *reductio ad absurdum* of them, in which the mathematical form of the poetry creates a space for a metaphysical content raging against its own futility, the result would be the actuality of Baudelaire's *The Flowers of Evil* and *The Spleen of Paris*. I have hinted above at the intellectual kinship between Kant and Baudelaire, but it would perhaps be advisable to make it more explicit, albeit briefly, before I turn directly to my interpretation of Baudelaire's poetry.

Baudelaire was a disciple, and acclaimed translator, of Edgar Allen Poe, who oriented himself in opposition to the New England Transcendentalists, who derived their philosophical program from Coleridge, who by way of the German Idealist philosopher Friedrich Schelling with a disciple of Kant (Hall, 2017). Thus, insofar as Baudelaire sided was the "Dark Romantic" Poe against the (bright?) "Romantic" Schelling, Baudelaire can be fruitfully placed in a position of oppositional indebtedness to Kant. It in this way that I argued, in my Comprehensive Examination paper, that Baudelaire can be meaningfully described as "belonging" to Kant. Having telescoped this genealogy, I turn now to the text of Baudelaire's *The Flowers of Evil* (1963).

According to its first poem, the largest flower in this garden, the greatest of all evils, is "Boredom" [*Ennui*]. Dedicated to the "Hypocrite reader—my semblance—my brother!" the speaker of this first poem claims that, of the "monsters" "of our vices/There is one most ugly, nasty and foul!," the "delicate monster" of boredom. The word *ennui*, and its associated parts of speech, appear many times in *The Flowers of Evil*, including five times in the longest poem of the book, "The Voyage." And if one accepts the editor's footnote claim that the word "spleen" "meant boredom to the Romantics," then ennui also becomes, by logical substitution, the title of another poem in the collection (the theme of which is, aptly, boredom). Boredom also becomes, by this same substitution, part of the title of *The Spleen of Paris*.

Ennui is also at issue in "The Albatross," which is probably the best-known in the entire collection. In three stanzas, "The Albatross" describes the crew of a ship who capture and bind on deck an albatross which has been following the ship in its voyage. The bird, a majestic "king of the blue" in the sky, becomes "comic and ugly," its "large white wings" described as "oars dragging at their sides" while grounded aboard ship (Baudelaire, 1963: 24). The fourth stanza makes an analogy between the albatross and the poet in the world which suggests that the world in question is that of the post-Kantian nineteenth century in particular:
— The Poet: semblance of prince of the clouds
— Haunts tempest, makes light of the archer;
— Exiled on the soil in a booing milieu,
— His giant's wings disallow walking (Ibid.).[5]
The poetic albatross here, like the poets in the wake of Kant's first *Critique*, finds himself banished from his home in the sky, the "beauty of the air" that could be the original derivation of Baudelaire's family name.[6] This seafaring imagery

also calls to mind one of the most poetic passages of the first *Critique*, near the end of the "Transcendental Analytic" (Kant's constructive account of reason's theoretical employment), and right before the "Transcendental Dialectic" (Kant's negative account of reason's overreaching theoretical employment). There, Kant compares the properly critiqued reason to "an island," which Kant terms "the land of truth—enchanting name!" (Kant, 1929: 257) The passage continues as follows:

> surrounded by a wide and stormy ocean, the native home of illusion, where many a fog bank and many a swiftly melting iceberg give the deceptive appearance of farther shores, deluding the adventurous seafarer ever anew with empty hopes, and engaging him in enterprises which he can never abandon and yet is unable to carry to completion. (Ibid.)

Kant's point here is that the theoretical "island" circumscribed by his *Critique* is the only stable, inhabitable home of metaphysical speculation, all others being illusory or at best temporary. Baudelaire's poet, however, does not want to be arrested on any *terra* whatsoever, *firma* or otherwise. The poet wants the clouds.

As this parallel suggests, "The Albatross" could easily be incorporated as a complementary reading assignment along with selections from Kant's *Critique of Pure Reason*. One could prompt one's students, before doing the reading, to think about possible relations between the two texts and authors, and perhaps to imagine a hypothetical conversation between Kant and Baudelaire. Better still, one could stage a performance exercise during class discussion, after the reading has been completed, in which two student volunteers sit in front of the class and do their best to play devil's advocates for the poet and prose philosopher, respectively.

In the penultimate poem from *The Flowers of Evil*, "The Abyss," Baudelaire references the French mathematician and philosopher Blaise Pascal. In the poem's last line, having just described his mind's vertigo and longing for nothingness, the speaker exclaims as follows: "Ah! No never to be at the end of Numbers and Beings!" (Baudelaire, 1963: 114). Thus, here at the end of the first section of Baudelaire's *Flowers of Evil*, one finds again numbers and being, mathematics and metaphysics, as well as the two primary subjects of Kant's first *Critique*, creatively united by Baudelaire in a mathematically beautiful expression of metaphysical rage. Interestingly, immediately after this last conventional poem, in Feltham's combined edition of *The Flowers of Evil* and *The Spleen of Paris*, Baudelaire does in a sense come to "the end of Numbers." As indicated in its subtitle, *Poems in Prose*, the mathematical meter and rhymed verse of *The Flowers of Evil* comes to its end. These prose poems, unlike the verse poems and their ungainly albatross, can walk comfortably and beautifully. It is in these prose poems, finally, that one encounters the famous original Baudelairean figure of the *flâneur*, so important to, among others, Water Benjamin (1892–1940). The *flâneur* can be interpreted as Baudelaire's philosophical challenge to the Kantian metaphysical boredom that afflicted the nineteenth century.

For reasons of space, I will defer that interpretation to a separate inquiry. For now, I limit myself to the observation that Baudelaire is centrally concerned with issues of freedom. Similarly, Kant called freedom the "keystone" of his entire philosophy, the gravity underneath his Copernican revolution of thought. But in the century following Kant's three *Critiques*, as my reading of Baudelaire suggests, the freedom Kant claims to offer appears insufficient, bearing a harsh remainder of unfreedom. For Baudelaire, as I have tried to show above, the epistemology of Kant's first *Critique*, in drastically limiting our certain knowledge to the natural sciences, results in profound boredom for communities forced to consider metaphysical questions at their leisure.

Put differently, Baudelaire captures, through the *flâneur*, the restlessness of a mind trapped in a world whose boundaries have already been rigidly defined by Kantian minds. And in this restless walking, I detect a symptom of this lingering Kantian unfreedom, in connection to the most famous aspect of Kant's own practice: his methodical daily walks. (His Königsberg neighbors famously joked that these walks were so rigidly timed that they could set their clocks based on the time that he passed by their houses.) In Baudelaire's case, the bored *flâneur*'s walk is a restless search for the stimulation denied to poetic thought by Kant's critical philosophy. Baudelaire's *flâneur* reunites what Kant divides in his first *Critique*, including the division between theoretical reason and practical reason, theory and practice, Kant's philosophical theories and his practice of walking.

To summarize, the way in which Baudelaire "belongs" to Kant lies in the way he takes the threads that Kant teases apart, and starts to reweave them together, in preparation for the major projects of reunion in the twentieth century (including the labor movement). For Baudelaire, like Kant, walking is vital to his practice. But unlike Kant, Baudelaire also articulates walking as a vital theme in his writing. He does so, moreover, specifically in relation to the Kantian theme of freedom. In Baudelaire, walking is both theorized and practiced, walking toward what was missing in both Kant's eighteenth and his own nineteenth centuries: the practice of freedom. In this way, incorporating Baudelaire's poetry into a philosophy class assignment on Kant's first *Critique* has the additional benefit of opening the important discussion about the thorny relationship between theoretical and moral philosophy, in Kant and beyond.

3   Conclusion

I will now briefly recapitulate my method of "empowering poetic defiance," paraphrased in terms of the insights from my preceding interpretation of Baudelaire vis-à-vis Kant. Beginning with the first step, the overcoming of my own poetic self-loathing was a necessary condition for, among other things, the present chapter and this second section's interpretation. The second step of empowering poetic defiance is manifested in my enabling the propositional content of Baudelaire's poetry (i.e. that in his writing which can be translated or paraphrased into prose) to enter a conflictual dialogue with the prose of Kant's first *Critique*. When confronted with the fact that both Kant and Baudelaire write of "vice," "evil," "art," etc., I proceeded from the strategic assumption that they are writing of shared phenomena in a shared world. The third step is manifested in my attentiveness to the formal dimensions of Baudelaire's writings, including the mathematics involved in the conventional poetry of *The Flowers of Evil* and the major shift from that to the prose poetry of *The Spleen of Paris*. And the fourth step is manifested by my refusal to dismiss Baudelaire qua thinker—a refusal to pretend that I have no obligation, as an interpreter of the most important Germanic philosopher of the eighteenth century, to attend to the response to Kant by one of the most important French poets of the nineteenth century.

In light of these analyses, I ask the reader to join me, and our fellow poets, in solidarity with a defiance of the unfreedom we continue to become. For this unfreedom we unwittingly spread to our beloved students—even though they most deserve from us freedom.

Notes

1 For more on Kant's role, see Bahti (1987).
2 This, according to a legend referenced by the medieval author Pizan (2000: 61).
3 For more on this reading of Wang, see Hall (2016).
4 For more on Kant's constructivism, see Hall (2013).
5 I have modified Fowlie's translation.
6 The other most likely etymology for the name "Baudelaire" is "beam of the air," as in the midship beam of a vessel.

References

Anzaldúa, Gloria. (2012). *Borderlands/La Frontera*. San Francisco, CA: Aunt Lute Press.

Ayer, A. J. (1952). *Language, truth, and logic*. New York, NY: Dover.

Badiou, Alain. (2005). *Handbook of inaesthetics* (Alberto Toscano, Trans.). Stanford, CA: Stanford University Press.

Badiou, Alain. (2007). *Being and event* (Oliver Feltham, Trans.). London: Continuum.

Bahti, Timothy. (1987). Histories of the university: Kant and Humboldt. *MLN*, *102*(3), 437–460.

Baudelaire, Charles. (1963). *The flowers of evil and other works* (Wallace Fowlie, Trans. & Ed.). New York, NY: Dover.

Boethius. (2008). *The consolation of philosophy* (David R. Slavitt, Trans.). Cambridge, MA: Harvard University Press.

Christine de Pizan. (2000). *The book of the city of ladies* (Rosalind Brown-Grant, Trans.). New York, NY: Penguin.

Condillac, Etienne Bonnot. (2001). *Essay on the origin of human knowledge* (Hans Aarsleff, Trans.). Cambridge: Cambridge University Press.

Coogan, Michael D. (2007). *The new Oxford annotated apocrypha*. Oxford: Oxford University Press.

Dewey, John. (2000). *Experience and nature*. New York, NY: Dover.

Hall, Joshua M. (2013). Redrawing Kant's philosophy of mathematics. *The South African Journal of Philosophy*, *32*(3), 235–247.

Hall, Joshua M. (2016). Nerve/nurses of the cosmic doctor: Wang Yang-ming on self-awareness as world-awareness. *Asian Philosophy*, *26*(2), 149–165.

Hegel. (1977). *Phenomenology of spirit* (A. V. Miller, Trans.). Oxford: Oxford University Press.

Heidegger, Martin. (2001). *Poetry, language, thought*. New York, NY: Harper.

Ivanhoe, Philip J. (2009). *Readings from the Lu-Wang school of neo-confucianism*. Indianapolis, IN: Hackett.

Kant, Immanuel. (1929). *Critique of pure reason* (Norman Kemp Smith, Trans.). New York, NY: St. Martin's.

Kant, Immanuel. (1993). *Opus postumum* (Eckhart Förster & Michael Rosen, Eds.). Cambridge: Cambridge University Press.

Kant, Immanuel. (2002). *Critique of practical reason* (Werner S. Pluhar, Trans.). Indianapolis, IN: Hackett.

Milton, John. (2008). *The major works*. Oxford: Oxford University Press.

Nietzsche, Friedrich. (2001). *The gay science* (Josefine Nauckhoff & Adrian del Caro, Trans.). Cambridge: Cambridge University Press.

Plato. (1925). *Plato: Statesman,. Philebus,. Ion*. Harvard Cambridge, MA: Harvard University Press.

Plato. (1986). *Plato's sophist: Part II of the being of the beautiful* (Seth Benardete, Trans.). Chicago, IL: University of Chicago Press.

Rancière, Jacques. (1991). *The ignorant schoolmaster: Five Lessons in intellectual emancipation* (Kristin Ross, Trans.). Stanford, CA: Stanford University Press.

Schiller, Friedrich. (2004). *On the aesthetic education of man* (Reginald Snell, Trans.). New York, NY: Dover.

Shakespeare. (2003). *The tempest* (Peter Hulme & William H. Sherman, Eds.). New York, NY: Norton.

Soyinka, Wole. (2002). *Death and the king's horseman.* New York, NY: Norton.

The Bhagavad-Gita. (1986). *Barbara Stoler-Miller.* New York, NY: Bantam.

PART 6

Sociology

CHAPTER 11

Contextualizing Math and Poetry in Community College Courses

Impacts and Implications in Introduction to Sociology

Amy E. Traver

1   Introduction

According to the Community College Research Center at Teachers College of Columbia University, 68 percent of community college students in the United States take at least one developmental reading, writing, or math course in pursuit of their associate degree (Jaggars & West Stacey, 2014). These courses aim to bridge the gap between students' secondary-school learning and their college-level course work; essentially rendering students "college ready" as they endeavor in college. Unfortunately, while developmental education is estimated to cost American undergraduates more than seven-billion dollars a year, it is largely ineffective for those students situated closest to the line dividing mandated enrollment in developmental coursework from a passing score on a college placement exam (Ibid.). Additionally, students' enrollment in developmental coursework is frequently experienced as a significant barrier to college graduation, particularly in the community college context: only 28 percent of community college students who are enrolled in developmental courses—courses that are non-credit-bearing and often a pre-requisite for enrollment in credit-bearing courses—graduate with their associate degree within eight years (Ibid.).

One suggestion for improving students' college readiness and their developmental outcomes is the contextualization of basic reading, writing, and math skills in credit-bearing content-area courses across the disciplines. According to Elaine DeLott Baker, Laura Hope, and Kelley Karandjeff, there are two models for this contextualization: (1) stand-alone classroom practices, wherein basic academic skills are integrated into the curriculum of a credit-bearing content-area course taught by a faculty member in the discipline; and (2) linked courses or learning communities, wherein a distinct developmental course and a distinct credit-bearing content-area course are linked to promote student readiness through connected learning (Baker, Hope & Karandjeff, 2009). While both models require faculty innovation and flexibility, the first model—the contextualization of basic reading, writing, and math skills into stand-alone content-area courses—asks faculty to step outside of their disciplinary training, eschew traditional course topics and methods, and engage new content and instructional strategies for student success.

Significantly, when the aforementioned models' impacts are analyzed, such study tends to focus only on students' understanding and development of the contextualized basic skills (e.g. Perin, 2011; Parker, Traver & Cornick, 2017). What remains to be understood, however, are the impacts and implications of contextualization on students' learning in the aligned credit-bearing content-area courses, particularly under the first model. This chapter represents one such study. Drawing on data from students' end-of-semester reflections in two separate efforts to contextualize basic skills in Introduction to Sociology at Queensborough Community College (QCC) of the City University of New York (CUNY), the chapter lends support for contextualization—of math (herein referred to as "project one") and reading/writing (herein referred to as "project two")—while addressing the impacts of contextualization on students' understanding of sociology.

2 Project One: Contextualization of Elementary Algebra in Introduction to Sociology

As part of a larger pre-test/post-test control-group design study funded by CUNY's Community College Collaborative Incentive Research Grant Program (Parker, Traver & Cornick, 2015), elementary algebra was contextualized in Introduction to Sociology course sections across multiple CUNY community college campuses in the spring 2016 semester. Elementary algebra was central to this design because of CUNY's math remediation requirement. At the time of this writing, and for the majority of CUNY students, exiting mathematics remediation required passing an Elementary Algebra course with a score of at least 60 on the CUNY Elementary Algebra Final Exam (CEAFE) and an overall course average of 74 percent, with the CEAFE score worth 35 percent of the overall course grade.

Contextualization involved the creation of three modules that aligned elementary algebra with Introduction to Sociology course content. Each module was designed with two goals in mind. First, while each of the three modules aimed to grow students' math skills, this growth was secondary to their primary focus: the use of contextualized math to reinforce the learning outcomes of Introduction to Sociology. Second, each of the three modules was intended to unfold in the same manner and order: (a) students' completion of a pre-module homework assignment, which used CEAFE-style problems to review the math content for the module; (b) an in-class lecture, where students were introduced to the sociology concepts, theories, and examples that grounded the module; (c) students' group work on an in-class assignment, which used CEAFE-style problems to connect the previously-reviewed math content to this new sociological material; and (d) students' completion of a post-module homework assignment, which used CEAFE-style problems to reinforce their learning.

Each module was connected to one of three topics from the Introduction to Sociology course curriculum—social deviance, social inequality, and social change—and each module was implemented in a way that built on the previous module's math and sociology content.

- Module One contextualized proportions and percentages in the study of social deviance, specifically the analysis of changes in marijuana use across time in the United States.
- Module Two contextualized linear equations and models in the study of social inequality, specifically the analysis of student test scores across New York City public school districts.
- Module Three contextualized linear models and inequalities in the study of social change, specifically demographic changes in/to the population of the United States.

Students exposed to these modules were enrolled in Introduction to Sociology without a priori knowledge that the course sections were part of a study. As a result, they came to the study from a range of mathematical backgrounds (i.e., needing math remediation, concurrently registered in Calculus I, etc.).

3   Project Two: Contextualization of Poetry in Introduction to Sociology

As part of a larger control-group design pilot study funded by a Pedagogical Research Challenge Award through QCC's Center for Excellence in Teaching and Learning (Jacob, Traver & Kincaid, 2016), poetry was contextualized in introductory courses in three humanities disciplines at the college in the fall 2016 semester. Poetry was selected because of its flexible alignment with the goals and outcomes of both developmental reading/writing courses *and* content-area courses. For example, brief poems can be easily incorporated into content-area courses as additional readings; poems can be used as writing prompts and assigned as formal and informal writing assignments; poetry exercises can aid students' comprehension of their more traditional course readings; and, as a descriptive art form, poetry can help to extend students' developing vocabularies.

For the purposes of this chapter, contextualization involved the integration of poetry in the Introduction to Sociology course. To best understand this integration, it is important to note three central elements of the project's design. First, and similar to the contextualization of math in project one, poetry was used to reinforce the learning outcomes of Introduction to Sociology. Second, while the study section of Introduction to Sociology was not "writing-intensive," poetry was integrated into the course with the goals of that designation in mind; specifically, "to help students grow as writers while they learn course material." (Queensborough Community College, Office of Academic Affairs, n.d.). Third, poetry was integrated into the course section in ways that were predictable for students and consistent across the semester: as an instructional tool; a low-stakes in-class writing prompt; a means to reading comprehension; and as a formal expression of research findings:

– Poetry was used as an instructional tool to enliven course lectures throughout the semester. For example, in a lecture juxtaposing social structure and agency, the author used an excerpt of W. H. Auden's "September 1, 1939" to illustrate the powers of both.
– Poetry was used as a low-stakes writing prompt to encourage students to pause, digest, and express their understanding of newly-learned material in their own words. For example, in a lecture on social identity, students were asked to write a poem that began "I am ...." Although these poems were collected by the author, they were used to verify students' comprehension of the course material—not to evaluate their creative expression.
– Poetry was used as a means to reading comprehension as students read abridged versions of classic works of sociology by C. Wright Mills, Émile Durkheim, Karl Marx, and Max Weber. For example, students were asked to create a "Found Poem" out of their highlighted text in C. Wright Mills' "The Promise."
– Poetry was used as a formal expression of research findings in lieu of a traditional research report or paper. For example, after conducting a field experiment on social networks and helping behaviors, students were asked to represent their findings in both the form and the content of an "Experimental Poem."

As in project one, students exposed to these activities were enrolled in Introduction to Sociology without a priori knowledge that the course section was part of a study. Consequently, they came to the study from a range of writing backgrounds (i.e., enrolled in developmental writing courses, previously enrolled in developmental reading courses, concurrently registered in upper-level English courses, etc.).

4 Data

Project one and project two are part of larger research studies aimed at understanding the impacts of contextualization on a broader scale. While both studies include more extensive data collection and analysis protocols, this chapter focuses only on those findings collated from a shared end-of-semester reflection assignment implemented across the two projects in the author's relevant Introduction to Sociology course sections at QCC.

At the conclusion of both projects, all students in the participating course sections (two course sections in project one; one course section in project two) were asked to respond to a brief set of in-class reflective writing prompts. These prompts were designed to gather students' thoughts and opinions about the project in which they were involved, and to serve as the foundation for a final in-class conversation about the students' work and learning. Across the two projects' writing prompts, three reflection questions were shared; they are abbreviated below:

1. How are poetry (or math) and sociology related?
2. In what ways did the course contextualization impact your reading/writing (or math) skills?
3. In what ways did the course contextualization impact your understanding of sociology?

While all students enrolled in the relevant course sections were exposed to contextualization, not all students consented to participate in the research on that contextualization; this necessarily limited the number of end-of-semester reflections that were eligible for analysis in the larger research studies. Additionally, because of the focus and bounds of this chapter, only consenting students enrolled in the author's sections of Introduction to Sociology were analyzed. As a result, this chapter draws on 31 end-of-semester reflections from project one and 14 end-of-semester reflections from project two.

5 Guiding Research Questions

Guiding the author's analysis of students' end-of-semester reflections on the contextualization of math and poetry in the Introduction to Sociology course were the following three questions: (1) In what ways—similar and different—do students report that math/poetry are related to sociology? (2) In what ways—similar and different—does contextualization aid students' self-reported development of specific aligned skills (reading/writing; math)? (3) In what ways—similar and different—does contextualization impact students' self-reported understanding of sociology? Notably, these research questions parallel the reflection questions assigned to both projects' students.

6 Findings

Both projects' end-of-semester reflections were analyzed via content analysis. According to Babbie (2001: 305) content analysis involves "the study of recorded human communications" through "a coding operation" that "(transforms) raw data into a standardized form" (Ibid., 309). Open coding was used to identify emergent themes and commonalities across the three questions. As a result, the resultant emergent codes were sufficiently broad and inclusive to allow for multiple associations within and across the three questions and two projects (Snow, Morrill & Anderson, 2003).

6.1 *In What Ways—Similar and Different—Do Students Report That Math/Poetry Are Related to Sociology?*

Significantly, students in both projects described contextualization as relevant to the sociological perspective and their learning in Introduction to Sociology; however, there were similarities—and differences—in their understanding of this relevance.

First, students in both projects found contextualization relevant because math/poetry and sociology were seen to *share a focus*. Yet, in each case, that shared focus was different. Students in project one described math and sociology as similarly focused on trends and patterns in social life: "With time and data we can show trends in society and have a pretty good guess on how a situation is going and its trajectory. Math helps us predict that trajectory and helps us determine the constant." In contrast, students in project two described poetry and sociology as similarly focused on general social issues: "They are related because sociology is about the study of society and people as a whole, and poetry talks about issues that are within society."

Second, students in both projects found contextualization relevant because math/poetry were experienced as *tools for better understanding the observable social world*. Nevertheless, the nature of these tools was different. Consistent with their sense that math and sociology are defined by a shared focus on trends and patterns, students in project one described math as a means of collating evidence about society: "Because sociology is a scientific field studying the society at a macro-level ... the mathematic method and technology can help us conduct a survey of a big population with a sample, which gives us the evidence for a hypothesis." Students in project two, however, described poetry, itself, as a form of evidence: "Poetry helps us to see and understand peoples' views and thoughts of what is happening around the world."

Third, and finally, students in both projects found contextualization relevant because math/poetry were understood as *means for the expression of social reality*. Yet, there were significant differences embedded within this similarity, as well. Students in project one described math as a direct means for conveying the aggregate or collective in society: "Sociology deals with society (obviously) and in society there has to be a population. If there's a population, there are numbers, and that's where math comes in." Counter to this, students in project two described poetry as a means of self-expression, which, when aggregated, could also express the social: "When you write poetry, you're writing a 'life' into words. Lives make up society and that's what sociology is about."

6.2 In What Ways—Similar and Different—Does Contextualization Aid Students' Self-Reported Development of Specific Aligned Skills (Reading/Writing; Math)?

Students' reflective writings provide extensive evidence of the impacts of contextualization on their understanding, embrace, and development of the aligned skills. (for more information about these impacts in project one, see Parker, Traver & Cornick, 2017). Notably, this evidence is remarkably similar across the projects, with students expressing two reasons for contextualization's impacts.

First, students in both projects wrote that contextualization *grounded— or provided a rationale for—their need to learn and develop the aligned skills*. In project one, students were consistent in their assessment of sociology as a "real world" defense for the utility of math: "Sociological content helped my understanding of math because it made the experience a little more tangible; meaning that seeing math apply to my everyday life and my world made me connect with it." In project two, students described poetry as a reliable source of academic support, specifically in the realms of reading comprehension and creative expression: "Poetry helped me to understand the readings more in depth. The use of poetry gave my writing a more creative element to it."

Second, students in both projects reported that contextualization provided an *additional opportunity to practice and/or learn the aligned skills*. Students in project one seemed particularly appreciative of the added time to use their burgeoning math skills in context: "This class helped me do better at practicing certain math skills because we were able to take our time and really get to understand it." Similarly, while students in project two also seemed to benefit from more time-on-task, they were careful to note the language-extending benefits of writing poetry, specifically: "Writing poetry helped me to be more creative and to look for new words instead of using the same old vocabulary all the time."

6.3 In What Ways—Similar and Different—Does Contextualization Impact Students' Self-Reported Understanding of Sociology?

Students in both projects wrote that contextualization furthered their understanding of sociology, as well. Yet, while one such benefit was constant across the projects, two other benefits were specific to project one and project two, respectively.

First, as critical thought is a central feature of the sociological mindset, it is important to acknowledge that contextualization seemed to have a significant impact on the *critical thinking skills* of students in both projects. Students in project one described how their analytic ability—specifically their ability to ask and answer questions about society—improved with contextualization: "The math content helped me to think critically while I was collecting data, where I began making assumptions about why certain things in society are happening." Students in project two described a similar phenomenon; often referencing poetry's precision as a model for careful thought about social life: "Writing and reading poetry actually made me think over the topics and questions that were asked and not actually breeze through them."

Second, while students in project two were involved in four data collection and analysis activities (the results of which they conveyed in poetic form), it was only the students in project one who cited contextualization as central to their understanding of *sociology as a scientific discipline*. For example, students in project one wrote that math helped them to see sociology's relationship to the scientific method: "Math helped my understanding of sociology by making it easier for me to see and read data, to make predictions and guesses, and see problems in society." They also referenced contextualization in their description of sociology's focus on causation and correlation: "Because of math, I was able to understand maybe why things are happening, using the data to make connections about why one situation is affecting another." Math encouraged students' grasp of sociology's empirical nature, as well: "Math helped me put sociology into an understandable and more easily observable context." And finally, students in project one realized the provisional nature of society—and our understanding of it—because of contextualization: "Math helped my understanding of sociology by setting a base for the trajectory of any broad topic. Seeing that forces increase and decrease pretty constantly helps us try to account for change."

Third, while students in project one were introduced to both the sociological imagination and the distinct paradigms that shape sociological theories, it was only the students in project two who cited contextualization as central to their understanding of *sociology as a distinct perspective on the world*. For example, students frequently contrasted everyday thought with sociological thought, often using the phrase "outside the box" to describe the difference: "In sociology you have to think clearly and think about your environment and you have to think outside the box." Significantly, what seemed to help students conceptualize sociology in this way was their grasp of *poetry* as an equally distinct and valid perspective on the world: "Poetry helped me think more deeply and helped me look at different aspects of society in different situations."

7   Discussion

In general, students experienced the contextualization of math and poetry in Introduction to Sociology as authentic and productive. Firstly, they came to recognize that math, poetry, and sociology are similar in their focus on and utility in society. Students in project one found math to be particularly fruitful in identifying and predicting trends and patterns in society, collating and analyzing evidence in and of society, and conveying the experiences of social members in aggregate. Students in project two found poetry to be a significant form of social expression; a type of evidence that begins with the self but extends to illuminate the experiences of many in and across social moments.

Second, students reported that their basic reading, writing, and math skills improved through contextualization. Students in project one appreciated the real-world defense of math that sociology provided, and they benefited from the opportunity to practice their math skills in context. Students in project two described poetry as a reliable source of academic support; one that encouraged them to write, read carefully and think creatively, and expand and develop their vocabulary.

Third, and most relevant to this chapter, students reported that their understanding of sociology was enhanced by the contextualization of basic reading, writing, and math skills in the Introduction to Sociology curriculum. Students in both projects reported that contextualization helped them to think more critically about the topics at hand, encouraging them to ask/answer deep questions about their social worlds—and to do so with a particular precision of thought. Yet, students in project one emerged from contextualization with a different understanding of sociology's orientation than did students in project two. For example, when describing the impacts of contextualization on his understanding of sociology, a student in project one responded: "Math helped my understanding of sociology by giving the information a kind of shape. Math gave sociology a form to me." But, as evidenced by this student's further reflections, as well as the reflections of his classmates, this shape/form was distinctly positivist and quantitative; focused mainly on sociology's use of the scientific method, provisional and empirical natural, and interest in causation/correlation. Missing from this understanding, of course, is the discipline's focus on meaning and extensive reliance on qualitative methodologies and data.

In contrast, when describing the impacts of contextualization on her understanding of sociology, a student in project two responded: "Poetry helped me to look at society and texts from a different point of view." As evidenced by her further reflections, as well as the reflections of her classmates, this "point of view" was similar to that which is employed in textual analysis; focused mainly on the interpretation of meaning and experience, and no different from or more reliable than any other parallel or personal lens. Missing from this understanding, of course, is the discipline's empirical nature, reliance on the scientific method, and grounding in and focus on the aggregate.

In essence, students' impressions of sociology reflected their experience of contextualization; mapping on to one of the two branches of insight and scholarship that currently define the discipline, depending on the project. Students in project one saw themselves as engaged in a form of *positivist sociology*, which tends to: define society as "out there," focus on social action, and engage quantitative methods to measure and gather evidence on the macro level. In contrast, students in project two saw themselves as engaged in a form of *interpretive sociology*, which tends to: define society as a social construction, focus on meaning and understanding, and engage qualitative methods to answer "how/why" questions at the micro level. Significantly, a comprehensive introduction to sociology should highlight *both* branches of the discipline, not reiterate and reconstruct what might be defined as an unproductive and even artificial divide in the field. Thus, this author's future use of contextualization—whether directed by students' basic reading/writing or their basic math needs—will necessarily integrate features of both projects, and it will use these features to highlight *and* weave together the discipline's branches/foci for students' benefit.

8   Limitations

While the data analyzed in this chapter are part of two larger research studies, the sample of students who consented to share their end-of-semester reflections with the author is unbalanced and small: 31 students from project one contributed reflections, and 14 students from project two contributed reflections. Future research in this area should attempt to balance and expand the study sample. Additionally, in future research on contextualization, potentially significant study variables should also be unpacked. For example, while elementary algebra is the typical manifestation of developmental math, poetry is only one means by which content-area course faculty can help students improve their basic reading/writing skills. As a result, faculty might consider other methods—like creative writing and narrative non-fiction writing—of contextualization. Other potential variables of interest are participating students' and content-area course faculty members' confidence in their abilities along the aligned skills, as these might impact contextualization. Related to this is the support received by the content-area course faculty engaged in contextualization. For example, while a member of QCC's math faculty was a partner in project one, project two unfolded without a developmental English faculty partner. This necessarily led to differences in implementation of the two projects.

9   Conclusion

The contextualization of basic reading, writing, and math skills in credit-bearing content-area courses has been proposed as an alternative to traditional models of developmental education in community college contexts. While studies indicate that such contextualization can positively impact students' learning of the aligned skills, no known research examines the impacts and implications of contextualization on students' learning of the credit-bearing content-area course curriculum. This chapter draws on data from students' end-of-semester reflections in two separate efforts to contextualize basic skills in Introduction to Sociology at QCC-CUNY: project one, which integrated elementary algebra into the introductory sociology course, and project two, which integrated reading/writing through poetry into the introductory sociology course.

Across the two projects, students' reflective writings offer additional support for contextualization. Students report finding math and poetry relevant to the study of society, and they express appreciation for and success along the contextualized basic skills. Yet, contextualization also seems to have had an impact on students' understanding of the course content, with students in project one emerging from the semester with a keen understanding of sociology as a positivist discipline and students in project two emerging from the semester with a keen understanding of sociology as an interpretivist discipline. While each understanding is essentially correct, the strength of sociology—and the responsibility of the introductory course—resides in the discipline's position at the intersection of both. Consequently, and at least in the case of Introduction to Sociology, it is recommended that basic reading, writing, and math skills are contextualized together, as this will render the discipline understandable in its most complete, true form.

Acknowledgements

Project one and project two are part of larger research studies aimed at understanding the impacts of contextualization on a broader scale. Project one was supported by a CUNY Community College Collaborative Incentive Research Grant (FY16-C³IRG). Project two was supported by a QCC Pedagogical Research Challenge Award. The author gratefully acknowledges the collaboration of her study partners (Drs. Stuart Parker and Jonathan Cornick on project one, and Drs. Frank Jacob and Shannon Kincaid on project two) and the participation of QCC's students.

References

Babbie, Earl. (2001). *The practice of social research* (9th ed.). Belmont, CA: Wadsworth.

Baker, Elaine DeLott, Hope, Laura, & Karandjeff, Kelley. (2009). *Contextualized teaching & learning: A promising approach for basic skills instruction* (Completion by Design). Retrieved March 5, 2017, from http://www.completionbydesign.org/knowledge-center/resource/contextualized-teaching-and-learning-a-promising-approach-for-basic-skills-instruction

Jacob, Frank, Traver, Amy, & Kincaid, Shannon. (2016). *Poetry across the curriculum: A pilot study in the humanities.* New York, NY: Queensborough Community College.

Jaggars, Shana Smith, & West Stacey, Georgia. (2014). *What we know about developmental education outcomes.* New York, NY: Community College Research Center, Teachers College of Columbia University. Retrieved March 5, 2017, from https://ccrc.tc.columbia.edu/media/k2/attachments/what-we-know-about-developmental-education-outcomes.pdf

Parker, Stuart, Traver, Amy E., & Cornick, Jonathan. (2015). *What is the impact of an introduction to sociology course infused with quantitative reasoning modules on students' quantitative literacy, and how do these impacts correlate with students' math placement and course history?* Community College Collaborative Incentive Research Grant, CUNY, Office of the Vice Chancellor for Research.

Parker, Stuart, Traver, Amy E., & Cornick, Jonathan. (2017). Contextualizing developmental math content into introduction to sociology in community colleges. *Teaching Sociology, 46*(1), 25–33. Retrieved July 18, 2017, from http://journals.sagepub.com/doi/full/10.1177/0092055X17714853

Perin, Dolores. (2011). *Facilitating student learning through contextualization.* New York, NY: Community College Research Center, Teachers College Columbia University. Retrieved July 18, 2017, from https://ccrc.tc.columbia.edu/media/k2/attachments/facilitating-learning-contextualization-working-paper.pdf

Queensborough Community College, Office of Academic Affairs. (n.d.). *Writing intensive graduation requirement.* Retrieved March 4, 2017, from http://www.qcc.cuny.edu/academicAffairs/wiGraduationReqs.html

Snow, David A., Morrill, Calvin, & Anderson, Leon. (2003). Elaborating analytic ethnography: Linking fieldwork and theory. *Ethnography, 4*(2), 181–200.

Index

A Raisin in the Sun   98, 102–105, 109
Academic writing   xiv, 55, 60
American Dream   99–101
A Midsummer Night's Dream   88
Arcadia   98, 109, 110
Aristotelian poetics   87
Art   viii, ix, xii, xiii, 3, 6, 8–10, 12, 25–, 30, 32–35, 37, 44, 49, 55–61, 63, 86–88, 90, 94, 100, 103, 110, 132, 139, 155, 164
Arts integrated learning   xiii, 25–27, 30–32, 34, 37
Associate degree   161
Auburn, David   98, 105, 109
Autobiography   71, 77–79, 146

Bachelard, Rene   27, 28
Badiou, Alain   150
Barthes, Roland   94
Basic skills   162, 171
Brainard, Joe   78, 79
Brecht, Bertolt   98, 104, 105, 107, 111
Buchler, Justus   132

Center for Excellence in Teaching and Learning (CETL), Queensborough Community College   163
Churchill, Caryl   109
Cognitive linguistics   30, 31
Cognitive poetics   58, 59, 80, 81
Community college   xii–xiv, 26, 43, 51, 55, 64, 83, 116, 118, 143, 161, 162, 171
Composition   55, 60–62, 67, 71, 79, 84
Conscientization   84
Content analysis   166
Contextualization   162–172
Critical thinking   25–27, 29, 69, 84, 85, 168
Criticism of
  Hughes   98, 108, 109, 111
  Jemie   102, 103
  Kerns   101
  Lenz   102, 107
  Moran   100, 101, 105, 108
Critique of Pure Reason   153
Cultural invasion   82, 86, 93
CUNY's Community College Collaborative Incentive Research Grant Program   162

CUNY Elementary Algebra Final Exam (CEAFE)   162

Dawkins, Richard   87, 88
Deep reading   91, 92
Design   xiii, 3, 4, 16, 18, 20–22, 162, 164
Designed object   3, 4, 12, 15–22
Developmental
  education   161, 171
  math   171
  reading   161, 163, 165
  writing   164
Dewy, John   26
Discourse   xiv, 55, 56, 60, 66, 67, 87, 145, 147, 149
Diversity   99, 100

Eisner, Elliot   26
Ekphrastic poetry   8, 9
Elementary Algebra   162, 171
Eliot, Thomas S.   X
Empowering poetic defiance   141, 142, 144, 146, 148, 150, 155
Ethics   ix, 131, 133, 137, 138
Experimental poem   164

First World War   117–119, 125
First-year college writing   71
Flâneur   154
Flowers of Evil   151–155
Freedom   9, 50, 74, 79, 80, 101, 154
Freire, Paolo   82, 84, 86

Galileo   98, 104, 105, 107, 111
German Idealism   149
Glaspell, Susan   108, 109

Habits of mind   55, 68
Hansberry, Lorraine   98, 102–105, 109
Harlem   98–102, 111
Hebrew   4, 8, 17, 18, 20
Hughes, Langston   98–102, 111

Imagery   3, 25, 27–29, 32, 35, 58, 72–74, 77, 102, 110, 152
Imagination   27, 28, 33, 37, 43, 44, 46, 47, 49, 79, 121, 169

Inclusive pedagogy   84
Interpretive sociology   170
Introduction to Sociology   161, 162, 171, 172
Introductory philosophy classes   133

Kant, Immanuel   xiv, 132, 141, 143, 146–155
Key logics   86

Love Jones   73–75

Mathematics   viii, x, 98, 105–107, 109, 111, 137, 138, 146, 150, 151, 155, 162
Memes   xiv, 82, 84, 86–88, 90, 92
Metaphor   11, 15, 25–33, 36, 37, 48, 49, 56–58, 60, 74, 75, 91, 93, 119, 144
My Papa's Waltz   61, 63, 65, 67, 68

Nietzsche, Friedrich   136–138, 143, 144, 149

Object poetry   3, 4, 5, 7–12, 14, 15, 17–22

Paz, Octavio   28–30
Pedagogical Research Challenge Award   163, 172
Plato   131, 132, 135, 141, 143, 144
Poetic expression   3, 6, 10, 43, 133, 137
Poetic self-loathing   142–144, 148, 155

Positivist sociology   170
Prejudice   99, 100, 111
Proof   98, 105, 109

Rape of Nanjing   122–124
Reflection   17, 43, 45, 46, 47, 48, 67, 68, 76, 80, 86, 136, 137, 162, 165, 166, 170, 171
Remediation   162, 163

Seeger, Alan   119, 120
September 1, 1939   164
Shakespeare, William   xiv, 76, 77, 82–86, 88, 90, 91, 93, 94
Similes   100–103, 105
Spleen of Paris   152, 153, 155
STEAM   30
STEM   98, 106, 107, 109
Stoppard, Tom   98, 109, 110

The Council of Writing Program Administrators (NCTE)   55, 68
Thomas, Edward   115
Top Girls   109
Transfer   46, 49, 50, 61, 67, 69, 84
Trifles   108, 109

Writing assignments   47, 72, 73, 133, 163

www.ingramcontent.com/pod-product-compliance
Lightning Source LLC
Chambersburg PA
CBHW070330230426
43663CB00011B/2273